"The world was peopled
with wonders."

The origin of Wildsam comes from above, a
line of prose in the novel, *East of Eden*, written by
John Steinbeck. Six words hinting at a broad and
interwoven idea. One of curiosity, connection, joy. And
the belief that stories have the power to unearth the
mysteries of a place — for anyone. The book in
your hands is rooted in such things.

WILDSAM
FIELD GUIDES

First and foremost, thank you to all the good folks in New Orleans; you've been so welcoming to so many for so long—including me. As we researched this project, it was a pleasure to work with the Historical New Orleans Collection, Hogan Jazz Library at Tulane, and New Orleans Public Library; Char Thian Miller, for years of hospitality; Kristian Sonnier, David Olasky, Kate LeSueur, Samantha Alviani, Sara Roahen, Chris Hannah, Alex Lebow, and Rush Jagoe, for steering us in right directions; Anthony DelRosario, for Lester's story; Rien Fertel, Katy Reckdahl, Brett Anderson, for great storytelling; Scott Campbell, for your stunning illustration work; and Nathalie Jordi [and Oscar], for your wonderful co-piloting of this project.

We'd also like to give kudos to several works about the incredible world that is New Orleans: *Inventing New Orleans* by Lafcadio Hearn; *Fabulous New Orleans* by Lyle Saxon; *Why New Orleans Matters* by Tom Piazza; and *Unfathomable City* by Rebecca Solnit and Rebecca Snedeker.

WILDSAM FIELD GUIDES™

Published in the United States by Wildsam Field Guides, Austin, Texas.

ISBN 978-1-4951-1285-0

Art direction by Stitch Design Co.
Illustrations by Scott Campbell

To find more field guides, please visit www.wildsam.com

⋙ CONTENTS ⋘

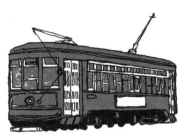

⫸ WELCOME ⫷

THERE'S AN OLD CREOLE PROVERB that goes like this: Tell me who you love and I'll tell you who you are. Earlier this year I read the line in a book of Louisiana folklore, and I jotted it down, thinking to myself, This sounds like New Orleans talking.

Then, a few months ago, I was sitting in Audubon Park, letting my mind rest after a few hours in the Hogan Jazz Library at Tulane. I had been studying the files of jazz ghost Buddy Bolden. Legendary on the cornet. Locked away in an asylum. Buried in an unmarked grave. Sitting there in the swollen heat of the park, I held two Xeroxed letters from the files. The first was from Bolden's mother, Alice, to the Superintendent at the State Mental Hospital. It read, handwritten and unpunctuated: "Dr will you please inform me of my sons health Charley Bolden from his mother Mrs Alice Bolden." She'd probably written it around 1910. The Superintendent had written a response, letting Alice know that her son "causes no trouble and cooperates well," adding too that while walking in the hospital, the patient "insists on touching every post...not satisfied until he has accomplished this." Bolden would never leave the asylum. No recordings of his music have ever been found.

As a trio of joggers ran by me, I heard the muted sound of a streetcar on St. Charles. A summer hum rose in the shade. *Tell me who you love and I'll tell you who you are.* I can't explain why, but the proverb rang out in my ears.

New Orleans is a beloved city. Though it bears its scars as deeply as any place in America, New Orleans is a place that is treasured. These pages are filled with people who prove this true. The river pilot steering ships up the Mississippi. The single mom hustling to get her girls to school. The sax repairman from Germany and the fisherman's daughter from Vietnam. The sign painter, the midwife, the chef.

They know the romance of New Orleans—mornings in the Quarter, bustling po-boy counters, Rebirth at the Maple Leaf. And they know well the city's wounds. Forgotten neighborhoods. Swollen prisons. The long disparity of race and class. As always, our hope with this field guide is to open up New Orleans as honestly as we can, with its stories and its people, its blessings and curses, who and what it loves. *-TB*

ESSENTIALS

TRANSPORT

STREETCAR
St. Charles, Canal
norta.com

....

BICYCLES
Bicycle Michael's
504-945-9505
bicyclemichaels.com

HOTELS

MARIGNY
Hotel Peter and Paul
2317 Burgundy St
hotelpeterandpaul.com

....

FRENCH QUARTER
Soniat House
1133 Chartres St
soniathouse.com

....

CENTRAL
Maison de la Luz
456 Carondelet St
maisondelaluz.com

....

GARDEN DISTRICT
Henry Howard Hotel
2041 Prytania St
henryhowardhotel.com

BUSINESS

MORNING
Satsuma
3218 Dauphine St
satsumacafe.com

CLIENT DINNER
Herbsaint
701 St Charles Ave
herbsaint.com

....

NIGHTCAP
Cane and Table
1113 Decatur St
caneandtablenola.com

CALENDAR

JAN	Sugar Bowl
FEB	Mardi Gras
MAR	St. Joseph's Day
APR	Crescent City Classic
MAY	Jazz and Heritage Fest
JUN	Cajun-Zydeco Festival
JUL	Satchmo Jazz Camp
AUG	Southern Decadence
SEP	Restaurant Week
OCT	Voodoo Fest
NOV	Treme Gumbo Festival
DEC	Celebration in the Oaks

BOOKS
↬ *The Moviegoer*
   by Walker Percy
↬ *Satchmo* by Louis Armstrong
↬ *Why New Orleans Matters*
   by Tom Piazza
↬ *1 Dead in Attic* by Chris Rose

FILM
A Streetcar Named Desire, 1951
When the Levees Broke, 2006
Twelve Years a Slave, 2013

ONE DAY

Morning in Audubon Park
Galatoire's lunch
Jazz on Frenchmen Street

....

WEEKEND

Arnaud's French 75
Cradle of Jazz tour
Sno-ball stop at Hansen's
Patois dinner
Preservation Hall, 10pm show
Café du Monde beignets

FOODWAY

King Cake
This pre-Lenten, sugary dessert
of Mardi Gras, colored purple,
gold and green, hides a plastic
Baby Jesus trinket inside its
doughy layers.

RADIO

WWNO 89.9
WWOZ 90.7

RECORD COLLECTION

King Oliver	*The Complete Set*
Dr. John	*In The Right Place*
Louis Armstrong	*Complete RCA Victor Recordings*
Mahalia Jackson	*The Best of Mahalia Jackson*
Wynton Marsalis	*Black Codes*
Trombone Shorty	*Backatown*
Rebirth Brass Band	*Feel Like Funkin It Up*
Professor Longhair	*Crawfish Fiesta*
Irma Thomas	*Soul Queen Of New Orleans*
Soul Rebels	*Unlock Your Mind*
Galactic	*Ya-Ka-May*
Lil Wayne	*Tha Carter III*
Sidney Bechet	*The Sidney Bechet Story*

ESSENTIALS

PROGRESS

- ☞ Over 1,300 restaurants operate today, up from 809 in pre-Katrina New Orleans
- ☞ One in three households participate in the city's voluntary recycling program
- ☞ Number of arts & culture non-profits is double the national average
- ☞ Katrina-ravaged areas have seen double-digit population growth since 2010, including Lower Ninth Ward
- ☞ More than half of neighborhoods reclaimed 90% population since 2005
- ☞ Five years after Katrina, Tulane received a record 44,000 applications
- ☞ The city murder rate was down 27% in the first quarter of 2014
- ☞ Startup business rate exceeds national average by 56%, from 2009-2012
- ☞ Tech and innovation jobs are up 28% in the city

CHALLENGES

- ☞ In 2013, a shooting occurred every 18 hours in New Orleans
- ☞ Per capita, Louisiana incarcerates more people than any state in America— by nearly double
- ☞ Among black males from New Orleans, one in 14 is in prison
- ☞ Obesity rates in metro area are five points higher than U.S. average
- ☞ Louisiana is losing 25 to 35 square miles of wetlands per year, more than the size of Manhattan
- ☞ Since 2010, Louisiana's oyster catch is down 27% from the average haul between 2002-2009
- ☞ According to the CDC, New Orleans ranks third among U.S cities for HIV case rates
- ☞ Average wages in New Orleans were 9% less than the U.S. average in 2013

STATISTICS

1 .... Fastest-growing U.S. city since 2007 recession, *Forbes*
90% .... NOLA students attending charter schools in 2014
$112 .... Median list price per square foot for New Orleans homes
27% .... Citizens living below poverty line, double the U.S. average
100 .... Miles of bikeways in New Orleans by end of 2014
800 .... Estimated age in years of the oldest live oak in City Park

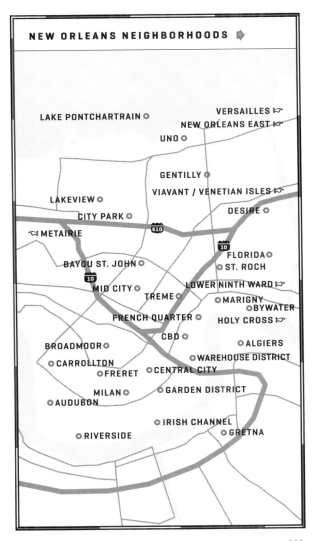

NEW ORLEANS NEIGHBORHOODS ➡

LAKE PONTCHARTRAIN ○
VERSAILLES ☞
NEW ORLEANS EAST ☞
UNO ○
GENTILLY ○
VIAVANT / VENETIAN ISLES ☞
LAKEVIEW ○
CITY PARK ○
DESIRE ○
◁ METAIRIE
610
FLORIDA ○
BAYOU ST. JOHN ○
ST. ROCH
10
MID CITY ○
LOWER NINTH WARD ☞
TREME ○
MARIGNY
BYWATER
FRENCH QUARTER ○
HOLY CROSS ☞
CBD ○
ALGIERS
BROADMOOR ○
WAREHOUSE DISTRICT
CARROLLTON ○
FRERET ○
CENTRAL CITY ○
MILAN ○
GARDEN DISTRICT
AUDUBON ○
IRISH CHANNEL ○
GRETNA ○
RIVERSIDE ○

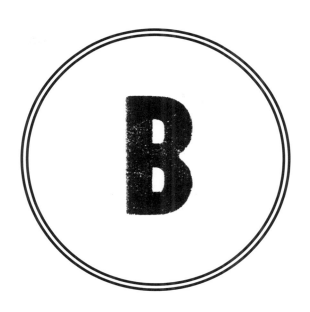

BESTS

A curated list of citywide favorites including po-boy shops,
beignet stands, seersucker, parade secrets, weekly jazz,
art galleries, movie theaters and more

»» FOOD & DRINK ««

For more classic cuisine and drinking spots,
see maps on page 56 and 68.

NEIGHBORHOOD CAFÉ

Patois
6078 *Laurel St*
West Riverside
patoisnola.com
Corner beaut near
Audubon Park,
boudin-stuffed
rabbit is a favorite.
....

OYSTERS

Pascal's Manale
1838 *Napoleon Ave*
Uptown
pascalsmanale.com
Bienville, Rockefeller
or Raw. Say hello to
Uptown T.
....

TAPAS

Mimi's
2601 *Royal St*
Bywater
mimismarigny.com
Manchego toast,
meatballs and the
"trust me" dish.

BEEF

Crescent City Steaks
1001 *N Broad St*
Bayou St John
crescentcitysteaks.com
Curtained booth
kind of joint, classic
cuts that sizzle.
....

SOUTHERN

Coquette
2800 *Magazine St*
Garden District
coquettenola.com
Elegant southern
leanings, adventur-
ous spirit.
....

SNO-BALLS

Hansen's Sno-Bliz
4801 *Tchoupitoulas St*
West Riverside
snobliz.com
Who knew ice could
be velvety? Look for
the line out the white
cinderblock building.

PO-BOY

Domilise's
5240 *Annunciation St*
West Riverside
domilisespoboys.com
Miss Dot, who
passed in 2013, and
her golden-fried se-
crets fill our Leiden-
heimer dreams.
....

GASTROPUB

Sylvain
625 *Chartres St*
French Quarter
sylvainnola.com
Understated,
laidback vibe—and
serving beef cheeks!
....

MODERN CAJUN

Cochon
930 *Tchoupitoulas St*
Lower Garden
cochonrestaurant.com
Donald Link carries
the Cajun torch.

NEW AMERICAN

La Petite Grocery

4238 Magazine St
Garden District
lapetitegrocery.com

Chef Justin Devillier's turtle bolognese with a fried soft boiled egg—whoa.

....

BISTRO

Herbsaint

701 St Charles
Warehouse
herbsaint.com

Another Link gift—and dark horse for best dark roux in Louisiana.

....

WHOLE FISH

Pêche

800 Magazine St
Lower Garden
pecherestaurant.com

New Beard-winning seafood grill, live-fire techniques over coals.

....

CREOLE ITALIAN

Mosca's

4137 US 90 West
Avondale
moscasrestaurant.com

Old Italian cook meets Louisiana fisherman—this 1946 classic marries both traditions.

VIETNAMESE

Pho Ga Quang Minh

2651 Barataria Blvd
Marrero
504-347-3553

At this cold-weather comfort, don't miss the slow-roasted, leg-in-bowl duck soup.

....

CLASSIC

Galatoire's

209 Bourbon St
French Quarter
galatoires.com

Epic tradition of the longest Friday lunches this side of old Europe. Men wear a jacket.

....

LATE NIGHT

Port of Call

838 Esplanade Ave
French Quarter
portofcallnola.com

Discover the combo perfection of a shredded-ched burger and loaded baked potato.

....

DAIQUIRI

Gene's

1034 Elysian Fields
Bywater
504-943-3861

Purple Stuff, All

Night Long, What the F—k. You know, the normal daiquiri flavors.

....

BEER BAR

Avenue Pub

1732 St Charles Ave
Lower Garden
theavenuepub.com

A *Draft* Top 50, their 42 taps will make you forget about Sazeracs for a night.

....

WINE LIST

Bacchanal

600 Poland Ave
Bywater
bacchanalwine.com

Buy your favorite bottle up front and pair with the house chef's superb stuff out back.

....

COFFEE

Revelator

637 Tchoupitoulas
Warehouse
800 Louisa St
Bywater
revelatorcoffee.com

Pourover lovers with design mojo; Bywater spot doubles as Caribbean cafe.

≫ SHOPPING ≪

MEN'S GROOMING
Aidan Gill
1026 Magazine St
Lower Garden
aidangillformen.com
Barbershop, dandy enclave—AG's makes you want to wear a new suit.

....

BOOKSHOPS
Garden District Books
2727 Prytania St
Octavia
513 Octavia St
New Orleans seems a rite of passage for American scribes.

....

ANTIQUES
M.S. Rau
630 Royal St
French Quarter
rauantiques.com
Fabergé eggs, estate jewelry, and a 125% buy-back policy.

JEWELRY
Mignon Faget
3801 Magazine St
West Riverside
mignonfaget.com
Fifth generation NOLA, collections draw from landscape and patina.

....

RECORDS
LA Music Factory
421 Frenchmen St
Bywater
Down the block from Spotted Cat and dba, open 'til 8pm.

....

HOME
Tara Shaw
1526 Religious St
Lower Garden District
tarashaw.com
Started with $14,000 and a plane ticket, now an Uptown institution.

LINENS
Leontine
3806 Magazine Street
Garden District
leontinelinens.com
Couture bedding and bath textiles, customized in-shop, sewn by artisan factory.

....

GROCERY
Canseco's
3135 Esplanade Ave
Gentilly Terrace
cansecos.com
Canseco's became city-famous when it re-opened super-quick after Katrina.

....

FRESH SEAFOOD
Westwego Shrimp Lot
Westbank Expressway
Stalls for rent sell freshest catch from Venice, Grand Isle.

LIFESTYLE

Sunday Shop

2025 Magazine St
Lower Garden District
sundayshop.co

Breezy shop
with global finds,
Moroccan rugs and
Guatemalan textiles.

....

LIQUOR

Keife & Co.

801 Howard Ave
Warehouse
keifeandco.com

Single barrels, arti-
sanal varieties, agéd
top-shelfers—and
free delivery for
$50 orders.

....

WINE

Hopper's Carte
des Vins

5601 Magazine St
Audubon
hopperscartedesvins.com

After nearly three
decades in wines,
Ric Hopper won't
put a bad bottle in
your hand.

....

SEERSUCKER

Rubenstein's

102 St Charles Ave
CBD
rubensteinsnewor-
leans.com

Made-to-measure
haberdashery since
before the Great
Depression, as
iconic as it gets.

....

FARMERS

Crescent City
Farmer's Market

Citywide
crescentcityfarmers-
market.org

Tuesday, Wednes-
day, Thursday and
Saturday. Fresh
and local.

....

CIGARS

Mayan Import
Company

3000 Magazine St
French Quarter
504-269-9000

Shined-up loaf-
ers. A hat from
Meyer's. Now, time
to light up a fresh
stogie.

....

GARDEN

Perino's

3100 Veterans Blvd
Metairie
perinos.com

Growing their own
blooms since 1955,
including some in-
credible "Louisiana
super plants."

COOKBOOKS

Kitchen Witch

1452 North Broad St
7th Ward
kwcookbooks.com

Wall-to-wall food
discoveries in a tee-
ny tiny, 180-years-
young building.

....

WIGS

Fifi Mahony's

934 Royal St
French Quarter
fifimahonys.com

A heaven for the
flashy, this empo-
rium is Mardi Gras
year-round.

....

SHADES

Krewe

1818 Magazine St
Lower Garden District
krewe.com

Eye-catching
styles befitting
jazz sounds on a
sunny day.

....

BOUTIQUE

Saint Claude
Social Club

1933 Sophie Wright Pl
Lower Garden District
saintcluadesocialclub.com

Dressing up with
avant-garde, colorful
panache.

⟫ ACTION ⟪

MOVIE THEATER
The Prytania
5339 Prytania St
Lower Garden
Not the fanciest
digs, plays indie
laurel-winners—
plus BYOB!
....

PLAYHOUSE
Saenger Theater
1111 Canal St
French Quarter
saengernola.com
A $40 million reno
brought grand dame
back with a 2,000-
pipe organ.
....

NATURE PRESERVE
Jean Lafitte
6588 Barataria Blvd
504-689-3690
Try Barataria Pre-
serve, full of swampy
waterways and
elevated boardwalks.

MUSEUM
Ogden Museum of
Southern Art
925 Camp St
CBD
ogdenmuseum.org
Icons such as Ida
Kohlmeyer and Cle-
mentine Hunter.
....

HISTORY
Historic New
Orleans Collection
533 Royal St
French Quarter
hnoc.org
Free exhibits in
a stunning brick
townhouse.
....

COOKING CLASS
Langlois
1710 Pauger St
Marigny
langloisnola.com
Whip up the NOLA
classics on site.

SAINTS BAR
Marky's
Bywater
640 Louisa St
Sometimes you just
want a long bar, cold
High Life's and
Drew Brees in hi-def.
....

GYM
New Orleans
Athletic Club
222 N Rampart St
French Quarter
Boxing ring, lap
pool, rooftop
yoga—all with a
pink-marble luxury.
....

RUNNING
Audubon Park
6500 Magazine St
Uptown
A few laps among
the dripping oaks,
then breakfast at the
Clubhouse Cafe.

Treme Brass Band
Tuesday at dba
618 Frenchmen St
Marigny
Toss-up! Other fave
is Kermit Ruffins at
Bullet's.

....

ANYNIGHT MUSIC

Spotted Cat
623 Frenchman St
Marigny
spottedcatmusicclub.com
Raucous tunes spill-
ing out, Jazz Vipers,
Washboard Chaz.

....

KIDS

City Park
1 Palm Dr
Lakeview
neworleanscitypark.com
Storyland play-
ground, the hand-
carved carousel,
beignets from Morn-
ing Call. Yippee!

....

REDFISHING

Giant Reds
7821 Sycamore St
Uptown
giantreds.com
Louisiana's
classic catch on a
flyrod with the state
record-holder him-
self, Gregg Arnold.

DANCE PARTY

Hi Ho Lounge
2239 St Claude Ave
Bywater
@djsoulsister
Ten years of the
"Hustle"—funk,
Afrobeat, reggae
vinyl spontaneity on
Saturday nights.

....

FOOD FESTIVAL

Oak Street Po-Boy
poboyfest.com
Heavyweight title of
city sandwich artists,
30+ makers and
50,000 eaters. Yum.

....

AIRBOAT TOUR

Cajun Pride
Swamp Tours
LaPlace, LA
cajunprideswamp-
tours.com
Up-close encoun-
ters with alligators
and water fowl.

....

GAY BAR

The Country Club
634 Louisa St
Bywater
thecountryclubnewor-
leans.com
Part bar-restaurant,
part saltwater-pool-
side hang [clothing
optional], all fun.

PRIVATE DINNER

Mosquito
Supper Club
mosquitosupperclub.com
Book a "houseboat
supper" for 8 friends
with the Louisiana
pop-up dinner ex-
pert, Melissa Martin.

....

CHEAP

Algiers Ferry
Foot of Canal St
Downtown
nolaferries.com
Two bucks to cross
the Mississippi. A
beautiful view often
forgotten about.

....

DAY PARADE

Zulu
kreweofzulu.com
African-American
jubilee since 1909
with tropical theme,
Satchmo was a
former king.

....

NIGHT PARADE

Muses
Lower Garden
District
kreweofmuses.org
All-lady krewe,
Thursday night
before Mardi Gras,
bedazzled shoes are
coveted throws.

» EXPERTISE «

BARBERSHOP

Mr. Chill's First Class Cuts
2734 S Carrollton Leonidas
504-861-7530
Super laid-back atmosphere with top notch taper fades and top shelf whiskey.

....

MARCHING BAND

Landry-Walker HS
1200 L B Landry landry-walker.org
Tough call with St. Augustine, the 100-plus Orange Crush band wins the battle.

....

WEATHER

Margaret Orr
@MargaretOrr
Chief meteorologist for WDSU News, born and raised in NOLA.

INNOVATION

Propeller
4035 Washington Ave Central City gopropeller.org/ incubator
Ten-month fellowships for social enterprise from maternal health to urban farming.

....

SOCIAL GOOD

Café Reconcile
1631 Oretha Castle Haley Blvd cafereconcile.org
Student-led restaurant aimed at training a new generation of food professionals.

....

BLOG

American Zombie
theamerican-zombie.com

Investigative reports on the city, including the scoop that sunk Mayor Nagin.

....

JAZZ INSTRUCTION

New Orleans Center for the Creative Arts
2800 Chartres St nocca.com
Notable alumni include Harry Connick, Jr, the Marsalis kids and *Treme* actor Wendell Pierce.

....

MECHANIC

Cacamo's
2205 Bienville St Tulane
504-822-2770
Trustworthy and quick with a wrench. Plus, a great po-boy spot is just down the block.

GAS LIGHTING

Bevolo

521 Conti St
French Quarter
bevolo.com

Opened in 1945, iconic copper lamps still glow throughout the French Quarter.

....

BREAD BAKING

Leidenheimer

1501 Simon Bolivar
leidenheimer.com

Famous po-boy carrier, delivered all over town every morning, circa 1896.

....

FURNITURE

Matthew Holdren

matthewholdrende-
sign.com
@matthewhold-
rendesign

Sources reclaimed cypress and pine to build signature pieces, most on commission.

....

DIGITAL STUDIO

Canary Collective

thecanary-
collective.com

Web design and new media for Dirty Coast Press, Rock 'n Bowl, Gaia Herbs.

ALT NEWS

The Lens

thelensnola.org
@thelensnola

Non-profit newsroom founded in 2009 to cover city government.

....

FUNK

George Porter, Jr.

georgeporterjr.com

Bass impresario with The Meters, funk legend, Mondays at Maple Leaf.

....

FILMMAKING

Court 13

court13arts.com

Collective led by Oscar nominee, Benh Zeitlin, Beasts of the Southern Wild.

....

PHOTO

New Orleans Photo Alliance

1111 St Mary St
Lower Garden
neworleansphotoal-
liance.org

Three hundred photographers lead gallery exhibitions and edu-programs.

....

SHUTTERS

New Orleans

Millworks

3315 Magazine St
Central City
nomillworks.com

Spanish cedar devotees, the best in town for historic wood restoration projects.

....

COASTAL ECOLOGY

John Barry

johnmbarry.com

Author, historian and flood expert filed ecological lawsuit against oil companies in 2013.

....

TATTOO

Electric Ladyland

610 Frenchmen
Marigny

The best kind of trip memento and the biggest, most respected ink shop in town.

....

COCKTAILS

Wayne Curtis

wayne-curtis.
squarespace.com
@waynecurtis

Drinks columnist for *The Atlantic*, contributor to *IMBIBE*, best guy in town to buy a drink.

ALMANAC

A deep dive into the cultural heritage of New Orleans through timelines, how-tos, newspaper clippings, letters, lists, jazz reviews and other historical hearsay

JAZZ GREATS

Instrument	Player
Tuba	*Anthony Lacen*
Trombone	*Honoré Dutrey, Kid Ory*
Cornet	*Joe "King" Oliver, Buddy Bolden*
Alto Horn	*Isidore Barbarin*
Melophone	*Davey Jones*
Trumpet	*Louis Armstrong, Terence Blanchard*
Piccolo Trumpet	*Wynton Marsalis*
Pocket Trumpet	*Gary Bruce Hirstius*
Sackbut	*Jack "Big T" Teagarden*
Alto Sax	*Donald Harrison*
Tenor Sax	*Johnny Pennino*
Soprano Sax	*Sidney Bechet*
Sousaphone	*Philip Frazier*
Piano	*Champion Jack Dupree, Allen Toussaint*
Clarinet	*Barney Bigard*
Bass	*George "Pops" Foster*
Banjo	*Johnny St. Cyr*
Drums	*Louis Cottrell, Sr., Warren "Baby" Dodds,*
Composition	*Jelly Roll Morton*

RAMOS GIN FIZZ

First shaken [and shaken and shaken] by Henry Ramos in the late 1800s at his bar on Gravier Street, the fizzy NOLA concoction traditionally took twelve minutes to make. In his heydey, Ramos had 20 working barmen shaking them at a time. Below, a classic recipe.

- ☞ 1 teaspoon powdered sugar
- ☞ 1 jigger gin
- ☞ Juice ½ lemon and ½ lime
- ☞ 1 egg white
- ☞ 3 oz. orange flower water
- ☞ 1 ounce sweet cream

Combine seven ingredients in a shaker without ice and shake for one minute. Add ice and shake again for at least a couple of minutes [all twelve if you have it in you]. Strain and serve in eight-ounce glass. Fill up with soda water.

ARCHITECTURAL DETAIL

Term	Description
Abat-Vent	*roof extension, almost flat, cantilevered from the façade*
Alligatoring	*severe cracking and crazing of paint*
Appliqué	*applied ornamentation*
Bousillage	*construction method for walls using mixture of mud and moss between heavy timber posts*
Camelback Shotgun	*shotgun type house with a two story rear portion; a "Humpback"*
Colombage	*popular framing method in early colonial period using timber mortised and tenoned together*
Creole Cottage	*French Quarter house style in 1800s, as seen in Lafitte's Blacksmith Shop*
Double Gallery	*two-story houses with a side-gabled or hipped roof, asymmetrical façade*
Egg-and-Dart	*decorative molding alternating between egg and dart-shaped elements*
Faubourg	*French word meaning suburb*
Finial	*topping ornament of a roof gable, turret, baluster or post*
Footcandle	*the illumination unit produced by a source of one candle at a distance of one foot*
Garçonnière	*Creole outbuilding used as living quarters for the young gentleman of the house*
Hipped Roof	*roof with four uniformly sloped sides; maisonette*
Modillions	*small bracket-like ornamentation under the cornice of a classical entablature*
Parapets	*portion of a wall that projects above an adjacent roof surface*
Porte Cochère	*carriage- or passage-way providing access to rear courtyard*
Quoin	*stone, brick, or wood block used to accentuate the outside corners of a building*

FABULOUS NEW ORLEANS

Lyle Saxon, noted Louisiana writer and historian, published his timeless work, Fabulous New Orleans, *in 1928. And in addition, he commandeered the Federal Writer's Project WPA guide to the city in the late 1930s. A good friend and generous host to visiting literati [John Steinbeck was married in Saxon's French Quarter townhouse] and, himself an unsatisfied novelist, Mr. Saxon was [and is] a beloved reporter of New Orleans enchantment. Below, an excerpt from* Fabulous New Orleans.

We did not return through the square, but went down some narrow street leading away from the river, toward the center of the old city. The sunlight was sliding down the walls, and in the open windows and doors women were gossiping. Parrots in cages hanging in upper windows screamed with raucous voices. Boys whistled as they passed carrying baskets. Heavy doors swung wide on protesting hinges, showing long dark passages with sunlit courtyards beyond, where flowers grew and festoons of vines clung to mouldering walls. As we passed through the streets the negro women were washing the banquettes by the simple expedient of pouring pails of water in great swishes, careless of the legs of passers-by. Other negro women were scrubbing staircases with pounded brick dust—"reddenin'" they called it. An old negro woman passed by, dressed in blue and wearing a stiff white apron. She carried a covered basket and as she walked she cried monotonously: "Callas! Callas!" Orleans Street was a little wider than the streets which we had just traversed, and the houses stood shoulder to shoulder, each one with balconies of ornate ironwork which repeated themselves in shadows against the gray brick walls . . . The passage into which we had come was fully fifty feet long and perhaps fifteen feet wide. It was paved with blue-gray flagstones and the long unbroken walls were of mouldering plaster which had been tinted green at some past time, but which were now peeling off in places, showing purplish patches, and here and there a space where bare red bricks could be seen. The ceiling was high above my head and was crossed at intervals by large beams. At the end of the passage, seen through an arch of masonry, was a large courtyard in which bamboo was growing and where tall palm-trees waved in the sunlight. The court was surrounded by the walls of the house, and a balcony extended around three sides of it at the second floor. There was a fountain in the center with a number of small pots of flowering plants ranged around its brim. A tall white statue stood ghost-like at one end, surrounded by a tangle of vines. . . Across the courtyard, at the back, a narrow flight of stairs rose a full three stories, stopping now and then at small landings, then curving and continuing upward. The railing of the stairs was of faded green, and was twined from bottom to top with a magnificent wistaria [sic] vine, covered with purple flowers. The whole court was full of color, but so subdued these colors seemed against the vast gray walls that the whole was as dim as some old print that has mellowed with the years. And near the fountain— I had not seen him at first—sat an old gentleman in black, beside a small breakfast table laid in the open air. The sunlight glimmered on the silver coffee-pot, and upon his crest of white hair, and upon a goblet which stood on the white cloth beside his plate. Upon the edge of the goblet sat a green parakeet, dipping its bill into the water.

THE BLUE DOG

Louisiana artist George Rodrigue rocketed to fame with his 30-year series of "Blue Dog" paintings, all based on a spooky Cajun bed-time story called loup-garou. Many think of him as the city's Warhol. Visit the Royal Street Rodrigue Studio to see the evolution of New Orleans' favorite pup.

1984	First Blue Dog, based on Cajun legend of loup-garou
1989	Opens first French Quarter gallery
1992	Absolut Vodka full-page Blue Dog ad in USA Today
1997	Inaugural portrait for Clinton-Gore with Blue Dog
2000	Worldwide Xerox ad campaign uses Blue Dog
2001	Tribute painting for 9/11 with White Dog
2005	Prints raise $2.5 million for Katrina relief fund
2008	Sotheby's auctions Blue Dog for $170,500
2013	George Rodrigue, age 69, passes away on Dec 14

TENNESSEE WILLIAMS
A letter to Donald Windham

The Pontchartrain Apartment Hotel
New Orleans, La.
December 26, 1945

Dear Don:

The lovely wind-instrument just reached me and I want to tell you at once how enchanted I am by it, as you must have known I would be. In spite of its extreme fragility it arrived altogether intact, not a bit displaced or broken, and I have been wandering around my room with it, unable to set it down, as it tinkles and jingles. It will go in the brightest spot of my new Apartment which I move into tonight or tomorrow and which is a dream, all the windows being shuttered doors twelve feet high and with a balcony looking out on the negro convent and the back of St. Louis cathedral, easy sanctuary in times of duress. . .

I was going home for Xmas but fortunately all north-bound planes were grounded, which heaven-sent dispensation kept me here. Christmas day was one of those exquisitely soft balmy days that occur here between the rains in winter, felt like an angel's kiss. I spent it in the Quarter in the apartment I am going to occupy as the present tenant, moving out this week, was almost as fortuitous a discovery as the apartment itself. It was so warm that we had dinner in a patio and wore skivvy shirts and dungarees. This present tenant has an aged grandmother who is the all-time high in southern ladies innocence. She entered our room this morning at a very early and most inopportune moment and as she strolled by the bed she remarked, "You boys must be cold, I am going to shut these doors."
. . .My coffee has come up and I must get to work, though it is hard to take my eyes off the wind-instrument. . .

Best wishes for the New Year, and love,

Tennessee

HURRICANE KATRINA

Wrecking havoc in late August and early September of 2005,
Katrina was the costliest hurricane in U.S. history [$135 billion]
and the deadliest [1,836] since 1928.

Aug 24	Tropical Depression Twelve strengthens, named Katrina
Aug 26	Pathway changed from Panhandle to MS/LA coastline Governor Blanco declares Louisiana state of emergency
Aug 27	At 5 am, Katrina reaches Category 3 status Mayor Ray Nagin calls for voluntary evacuation, 5 pm
Aug 28	At 7 am, winds of 175 mph put storm at Category 5 Mandatory evacuation of Orleans Parish Superdome opened as "refuge of last resort" for 30,000
Aug 29	Eye of hurricane passes over city Levee breaches at 17th Street and Industrial canals Power goes out at Superdome Ninth Ward under 8-10 feet of water
Aug 30	Superdome ordered to be evacuated, takes 5 days
Aug 31	Eighty percent of city underwater, 53 levee breaches Infamous Air Force One photograph of President Bush Memorial Medical Center—no power, no water, 100 degrees
Sep 1	Bridge into Gretna blocked by armed police officers FEMA's Michael Brown tells CNN "no reports of unrest" Helicopter rescues continue, total up to 4,489 residents
Sep 2	Algiers man, Henry Glover, murdered by NOPD "Brownie, you're doing a heck of a job," Bush to FEMA's Brown
Sep 4	Police shoot two unarmed men on Danziger Bridge
Sep 9	Homeland Security blocks all media access, CNN files lawsuit
Sep 11	45 dead patients recovered from Memorial Medical Center
Sep 12	FEMA's Michael Brown resigns
Sep 15	President Bush delivers speech from Jackson Square
Sep 19	Hurricane Rita on horizon, second evacuation ordered
Oct 13	Over 600,000 refugees living in subsidized hotels
Nov 23	Over 6,500 adults unaccounted for, 400 bodies unidentified

MARDI GRAS INDIAN TRIBES

A list of traditional African-American revelers, past and present.

Apache Hunters

Black Eagles

Blackfoot
Hunters

Black Hawk
Warriors

Carrollton
Hunters

Cheyenne Hunters

Creole Osceola

Creole Wild West

Diamond Stars

Eastern Cherokee

Eight Bad Men

Fi Ya Ya

Flaming Arrows

Geronimo
Hunters

Golden Arrows

Golden Blades

Golden Eagles

Golden Sioux

Golden Star
Hunters

Guardians of the
Flame

Morning Star
Hunters

Mohawk
Hunters

Ninth Ward
Hunters

Original Yellow
Jackets

Red Frontier
Hunters

Red, White
and Blue

Second Ward
Hunters

Seminole Warriors

Seventh Ward
Hunters

Shabke Hunters

The Hundred
and One

Third Ward
Terrors

Troubled Nation

White Cloud
Hunters

White Comanche
Hunters

White Eagles

Wild Apache

Wild Bogocheetus

Wild Magnolias

Wild Soua-tou-las

Wild
Tchoupitoulas

Young Brave
Hunters

Yellow Jackets

Yellow Pocahontas

NOTABLE KREWES

Mistick Krewe of Comus	*In 1991, New Orleans passed an ordinance that required krewes to open their doors to all, regardless of race or gender. Historic Comus, along with Momus and Proteus, withdrew from parading rather than comply.......1856*
Krewe of Rex	*Formed as city recovered from the Civil War, they are originators of the official Carnival colors of purple, green and gold.......1872*
Zulu	*African-American krewe, whose king first paraded wearing a lard can crown and banana-stalk scepter to parody white Mardi Gras. Throw hand-decorated "golden nugget" coconuts.......1909*
Barkus	*All dogs dressed-up in costume.......1909*
Krewe of Endymion	*One of the "super krewes," defined by stunning visuals and technology. In 2013, they set a world record for the largest Mardi Gras float—330 feet long, 230 riders, $1.2 million to build.......1967*
Krewe du Jieux	*Krewe of Jews and the "Jew-ish" aiming to draw attention to the absurdity of Jews being historically excluded from Mardi Gras celebrations in New Orleans. Throw hand-decorated bagels.......1995*
Muses	*All-women's krewe that throws elaborately hand-decorated shoes.......2000*
'tit Rex	*Instead of massive floats that take up entire blocks, their floats are tiny, made out of shoe boxes pulled on strings.......2009*

"POSEIDON, KIND OF SEA, RULES OVER HOLMES BALL WITH MISS MCCABE QUEEN"

Times-Picayune
February 7, 1927

POSEIDON, King of the Sea, held sway with his queen over revelers at the D. H. Holmes Carnival ball last night in the Athaneum. The large ballroom was decorated to represent the meeting of the waves and the sky, the realms of Poseidon and of mortals, the tableaux carrying out the theme in attractive, colorful display. Poseidon was represented by Paul Bailey, the popularly chosen king, his queen being Miss Myrtle McCabe, whose royalty also was declared by acclamation. At 9 o'clock, the curtain rose upon the first tableaux of the Carnival pageant, a scene representing the ocean, bathing girls and a ballet and titled "Moonlight and the Waves." The ballet, presented by Miss Jeanne Ploger, caught the spirit of dancing waves and glittering moonlight and merged them into one. The second curtain rose on "The Rainbow Trail," an intricate figure presented by the Cotillion Club of eighty young women and twenty men. Ballet costumes of pastel rainbow hues and harlequins in the same lovely colorings came from right and left wings of the stage to form entrancing figures on the stage and then, a circle on the ballroom floor. Following the tableaux of the sea, Poseidon and his court were shown awaiting the queen and maids. Their arrival, announced by a royal bugler before the footlights, brought a crescendo of applause and preceded the grand march of the royal party and the maskers. The queen gowned in white and silver, with rhinestones and pearls for jewels, was a fitting complement to the green-mantled glory of Poseidon and his jewels of rhinestones and emeralds. Following the grand march, E. Davis McCutchon, captain, led the march of the maskers. [Excerpt]

"ROYAL REFULGANCE – CARNIVAL COURTS MEET"

New Orleans Advocate
April 5, 2014

During the apex of Carnival elegance and in a tradition-bound moment, four monarchs stood together on the stage set up in the New Orleans Marriott and acknowledged the ovations of their subjects, who were dazzled by the brilliance of the Rex and Comus royalty. Spotlighted for the Rex regality were the king and queen of Carnival, Mr. John P. "Jack" Laborde and Miss Carroll Irene Gelderman, daughter of Mr. and Mrs. Gregory Anthony Gelderman III. Comus, as the king of the Mistick Krewe of Comus is called, reigned anonymously, but his radiant queen was Miss Pauline Mason Ukrop, who answers to Polly, and is the daughter of Mr. and Mrs. Robert Scott Ukrop. Both queens have mothers who wore crowns for old-line Carnival balls. Year after year, there's a special thrill in the season's waning moments of the four astride monarchs as they sweep the scepters of the Rex twosome and the Comus queen, along with the cup of Comus, in sequence. Carnival hearts pound with delight. As she processed, the comely crowd could admire close up the gown of queen Carroll, a design by Suzanne Perron. Trumpet-shaped in cut, the regal robe was of gold tissue lamé and metallic tulle with features of radiant embroidery, alternating vertical bands, and brilliant encrustation. His majesty Jack Laborde was not masked, but bewigged, prompting a comment before his ride and reign that one of the things he most looked forward to on Mardi Gras was "having a full head of hair all day long." As the Comus queen, Polly Ukrop shimmered in a diamond-white and silver gown. Family jewelry—including a Victorian necklace first worn by Polly's great, great, great grandmother—completed the radiant ensemble. [Excerpt]

A LETTER FROM LOUIS ARMSTRONG

Evansville Ind.
September 25th, 1942,

I've done things a lot of times
And I've done them in a Hustle
But I break my neack [sic] almost every time
To write to my boy-Wm Russell,..
Lawd Today.

'How'Doo' Brother Russell:

:Man - you talking about a 'Cat thaw, been trying his 'damnedest to get this fine chance to write to you my friend it was'Mee. . . .My'Gawd. . . .I never thought that one man could be as busy as your boy Ol Satchmo Gatemouth! Louis Armstrong. . . .ha. . . .ha. . . .But 'Ah'Wuz'. . . .ha. . . .You talk about a guy being as busy as a one arm paper hanger with 'crabs...tee her—Dats Mee. . . .But I was just determined to let you hear from me"Gate. . . .

I also want to thank you for being so kind as to send me one of those fine books of yours, "Jazzmen" . . . .I've 'Scanned the ass off it already-and it's a Solid Sender. . . .Honest. It's undoubtedly the best book on Jazz-yet. . . .Theres none other that can 'Cut It in my estimation. . . .You really tells the folks what it's all about when it comes to really taking about New Orleans LA. . . .Yessir Mr Russell your book tells about New Orleans just the way I [personally] saw it when New Orleans was a New Orleans. . . .'Yarsuh . . . .Of course it's just the 'Remnants now. . . .tee her. . . .

Well Brother Russ, I'll have to do you like the Farmer did the Potatoe, I'll plant ya now-and 'Dig ya later. . . .tee here. . . .So take me slow and tell all of the Fans that ol Satchmo said to take it easy. . . .Also tell them—by the time you get this letter I'll have my Divorce from my third wife and I'll be on my way to the Altar with my fourth wife. . . .Which is the sharpest one of all of them. Yessir-Madam Lucille Wilson is gonna make all of the rest of the Mrs Satchmo's look sick when she walks down the Aisle with Brother Satchmo Armstrong looking just too-pretty for words with her little Brown

Cute Self. . . .Lawd today. . . .

Here's saying goodnight and God Bless you brother Russell...And if Lucille and I have more than one Satchmo—I'll name one of them Russell. . . .Your Name . . . .Nice? . . . .You see the first one will have to be named Satchmo Louis Armstrong Jr . . . Savy? . . . .ha . . . And believe me Pal—we're really going to get down to real—'Biz'nez this time. Catch on?— Oh Boy. . .

Am Redbeans and Ricely Yours,

[Signature] Louis Armstrong

SUPERSTITION AND LORE

Always burn the onion peels and you will always have money.

....

To hurt an enemy, put his name in a dead bird's mouth and let the bird dry up.

....

If someone has bitten you, put some chicken manure on the wound and all your enemy's teeth will fall out.

....

To make the chicken stay home, spit in its throat and throw it up the chimney.

....

To get rid of a man, pick a rooster naked, give him a spoonful of whiskey, then put in his beak a piece of paper on which is written nine times the name of the person to be gotten rid of. Turn the rooster loose in Saint Roch's cemetery. Within three days the man will die.

....

To drive a woman crazy, sprinkle nutmeg in her left shoe every night at midnight.

> *These superstitions were gathered by Louisiana writer Robert Tallant, who participated in the WPA Writer's Project in the 1930s.*

LOVE AND MARRIAGE

*In 1858, a New Orleans attorney named S.S. Hall stirred
a pot of scandal with his book,* Bliss of Marriage, or How
to Get a Rich Wife. *In it, Hall opined on love and court-
ship, and listed, in detail, the most eligible men and women
of deep pockets. The published ruminations incited six
reported duels. Hall soon left town for good.*

ON INDEPENDENCE "Most ladies like stormy courtships,
and when the heart of a man is too faint to assert his rights and
independence, he becomes an object of ridicule."

···

ON AMBITION "He who does not wish a lazy wife, had better never
marry a girl who sleeps till breakfast."

···

ON BLOODLINES "To see a young man making love to his cousin,
is the surest evidence of a weak and imbecile mind."

···

ON ASCENT "Man is like a kite, he requires weight to ballast and
buoy him up to higher and more aerial climes."

VOODOO CHARMS

A short list available in 1938

Love Powder, White & Pink .. 25¢	*Devil Oil* .... 50¢
Cinnamon Powder .... 25¢	*Luck around Business* .... 50¢
War Powder .... 50¢	*Lucky Jazz* 1.00
Controlling Powder .... 50¢	*Come to Me Powder* 1.00
Delight Powder .... 50¢	*Controlling Oil* 1.00
Gamblers' Luck .... 75¢	*Mexican Luck* .... 50¢
Dice Special 1.00	*Snake Root* .... 25¢

FLORA OF NOTE

Plant name	*Description*
Chinese Wisteria	*hanging lavender bouquets in April and May*
Dutchman's Pipe	*green tropical climbers known as Pelican plant; invasive*
Confederate Jasmine	*intoxicating, white-petalled vines overflow like bouffants*
Indigo Spires	*bold blue spikes, tough-minded through first frost*
Bougainvillea	*booming tropical billows with three blooms a year*
Arborvitae Fern	*pale green, lacy varietal, shady, moist home*
Banana Tree	*red, pink velvet and classic, bright green elephant ears*
Possomhaw Holly	*warty-barked swamp plant, shiny red berries*
Giant Blue Flag	*purple-blue iris is official state wildflower of Louisiana*
Wild Sweet William	*early summer blooms, lavender, white and blue*
Gardenia	*lustrous dark foliage, champion white flowers*
Angel's Trumpet	*poisonous pale purple to white, lemony scent*
Shrimp Plant	*pinkish-red flowers shaped like giant prawns*
Macho Fern	*balcony behemoths can grow six feet in width*
Mamou Plant	*early pop of red, natives used for bowel pain*
Toadshade	*perennial trillium, foul stench from inner flower*
Beautyberry	*metallic sheen on clustered berries, good for jellies*
Sweet Olive	*hints of orange-apricot induce heavenly deep breathing*
Spanish Flag	*five petals, brilliant red, known as 'Chinese rose'*
Honeybush	*sweet, sugary smell with leaves ready for tea steeping*

THANKING THE SAINTS

*Published in the "Personal" advertisements section
of the* Times-Picayune, *April* 1928.

THANKS to Sacred Heart of Jesus for favor granted. Mrs. T. O'Neil

THANKS to St. Jude for favor granted. Holy masses and publication promised. A Client.

THANKS to the Sacred Heart of Jesus, His Immaculate Mother, St Joseph, and St. Anthony for favors granted. Mrs. C.

THANKS to St. Rita and Little Flower of Jesus for special favor granted. Mrs. Charles H. Frantz, 920 Jena.

THANKS to the Little Theresa, Flower of Jesus and St. Jude. N. N. M.

THANKS to St. Michael the archangel, Our Lady of Prompt Succor, My Guardian Angel, my two little angels in heaven, Willie and Regina, also to Father Pro, the Mexican martyred priest for extraordinary favors granted me. W. T. L.

AM applying for a pardon or commutation of sentence. *JOHN LIGHTFOOT.*

NOT responsible for debts contorted by my wife, George G. Moll.

THANKS to St. Anthony for finding silver. Promised publication. M. B. V.

PROMISED PUBLICATION. Thanks to Our Lady of Prompt Succor for saving city from flood last May. M. B. V.

ED—Am trying to make Tuesday as usual. Clara.

I AM NOT responsible for any debts contorted by my wife. STEVE CESKA.

ANY member of Col. Dreure's Orleans Guards during Civil war remembering Charles L. F. Platz, please phone his widow. Uptown 2176-W.

THANKS to St. Janaarius and Companions for favor. Mrs. L. H.

THANKS to St. Theresa, Little Flower of Jesus, for safe return of my dog. Mrs. F. F. P.

THE DEAD VOUDOU QUEEN
Marie Laveau's Place In The History Of New-Orleans

The New York Times
June 23, 1881

NEW-ORLEANS. — Marie Laveau, the "Queen of the Voudous" died last Wednesday at the advanced age of 98 years. To the superstitious creoles Marie appeared as a dealer in the black arts and a person to be dreaded and avoided. Strange stories were told of the rites performed by the sect of which Marie was the acknowledged sovereign. Many old residents asserted that on St. John's night, the 24th of June, the Voudou clan had been seen in deserted places joining in wild, weird dances, all the participants of which were perfectly nude. The Voudous were thought to be invested with supernatural powers, and men sought them to find means to be rid of their enemies, while others asked for love powders to instill affection into the bosoms of their unwilling or unsuspecting sweethearts. Whether there ever was any such sect, and whether Marie was ever its Queen, her life was one to render such a belief possible. Besides knowing the secret healing qualities of the various herbs which grew in abundance in the woods and fields, she was endowed with more than the usual share of common sense, and her advice was oft-times really valuable and her penetration remarkable. Adding to these qualities the gift of great beauty, no wonder that she possessed a large influence in her youth and attracted the attention of Louisiana's greatest men and most distinguished visitors. In [the Laveau mansion] Marie received the celebrities of the day. Lawyers, legislators, planters, merchants, all came to pay their respects to her and seek her offices, and the narrow room heard as much wit and scandal as any of the historical salons of Paris. There were business men who would not send a ship to sea before consulting her upon the probabilities of the voyage. [Excerpt]

BETSY SURVIVOR RELATES HORROR OF NEW ORLEANS FLOOD DISASTER

September 13, 1965

NEW ORLEANS, La. *[AP]*—Willie Brown had returned to his home on Reynes Street last Thursday night and was relaxing in an easy chair.

For the last 20 years, Willie has been a chef at a restaurant across from Charity Hospital. He's a round little man of 50 who wears glasses and moves at an easy gait because of heart trouble.

He's unathletic looking and can't swim.

"Sure I was worried about Betsy but I had been through hurricanes before," he said. "I figured I could go through another one."

As Willie remembers, it was about 8:30 p.m. when he put his glasses and wallet on top of this television set and dozed off.

"I didn't have any juice [electricity] so I had no TV," he said. "I had no trouble falling asleep."

Willie might have spent all night in his chair—except he was suddenly awakened an hour later.

"I felt something cold, looked down and there I was with water in my lap," he said.

"I jumped out of the chair, raced to the back door and opened it. Swoosh! In came the water. It had me around the shoulder and, for a moment, I was about to go crazy.

"All I could think of was me and Lady—that's my dog. I grabbed Lady and I really can't tell you how but I climbed up an iron railing and made it on top of my roof."

Willie figures the top part of his roof is almost 15 feet high.

"By the time I got up there," he says, "the water was lapping at my pants and the wind was pouring all around. It was all I could do to keep Lady under my arm and put my fingernails into the tar paper.

"Three times during the night I was blown off and I had to claw my way back up to the top."

Willie Brown's battle for life lasted 19 hours—ending at 5:30 p.m. Friday when a motorboat plucked him and several of his neighbors from their rooftop refuge.

"God it was like one big swimming pool as far as the eye could see," says Willie. "There were people I knew, women, children, screaming and praying."

The night of terror as Betsy was whipping through with 125 miles an hour winds was bad enough. But even though the wind had slowed, daylight brought a picture forever etched in Willie Brown's memory.

"It must have been around eight in the morning when a lady who lives down the block floated past, with her two children right alongside. I guess the wind was too much or I guess she just gave in."

Along with the bodies were a number of deadly snakes and every time he saw one Willie's fingers dug deeper in the tar paper.

"I guess you can say I lost everything but my life," says Willie. "But that makes me a lot luckier than a lot of folks. You can always get some clothes and earn money to buy food and find a place to stay. So I sure can't complain. You have thousands a lot worse off than me."

COOKBOOKS

THE PICAYUNE'S CREOLE COOK BOOK
Fascinating to see how [little] things change, 1901

RIVER ROAD RECIPES
Dog-eared Baton Rouge home-cook series, 1950

THE NEW ORLEANS RESTAURANT COOKBOOK
The institutions. Commander's, Arnaud's, more, 1967

CREOLE FEAST
African-American masters share the classics, 1978

LOUISIANA KITCHEN
Prudhomme puts Cajun spice on the map, 1984

THE LITTLE GUMBO BOOK
More than three dozen ways to roux, 1987

THE DOOKY CHASE COOKBOOK
Leah Chase's soulful story and recipes, 1990

GALATOIRE'S COOKBOOK
Delicious recipe secrets spilled, 140 in all, 2005

REAL CAJUN
Donald Link's Beard Award-winner, 2009

LAWS

RESOLVED, That it shall be the duty of any officer, Commissary of police, and of any man of the city guard; and it shall be lawful for any individual to kill the hogs running at large in the streets, provided, however, that no fire arms be used.

BE IT FURTHER RESOLVED, That the hogs killed as aforesaid shall become the property of the person or persons arresting or killing the same.

Passed September 13, 1834.—Not rejected.

....

Any person who shall tame or break any horse or horses, mule or mules, either by riding the same, or harnessing the same to any dray, cart, tumbrel or carriage whatseoever, in the streets or public ways of the City and suburbs, shall be condemned to a fine from ten to twenty-five dollars, for each contravention.

Passed on December 30, 1833.—Not rejected.

....

RESOLVED, That in the future it shall be lawful to sell oysters agreeably to existing ordinances, from the 15h September to the 15th of April, in each year.

Passed on September 6, 1834—Not rejected.

....

RESOLVED, That from and after the publication of the present resolution, it shall not be lawful to beat the drum or base drum in the houses or yards of the City, so as to disturb the quietness of the neighbors, under the penalty of a fine of ten dollars each. Provided, also, That the present provision shall apply to all parts of the City and suburbs, except that part of Girod street below Baronne street.

Approved, April 10, 1835.

RACE

*Over the centuries, a cultural melting pot of racial divisions created
a complicated vocabulary for New Orleans life. Here, a historic
sampling from* A Creole Lexicon *by Jay Dearborn Edwards
and Nicholas Kariouk Pecquet du Bellay de Verton.*

Designation	Definition
Nègre[sse]	a black-skinned person or a person of purely African descent
Sacatra	an individual with seven parts African blood and one part European blood
Moreno[a]	a dark-skinned black person
Marabou	the offspring of a mulatto and a griff; a person with five-eights African blood
Mulâtre[sse]	the child of a blanc and a negré
Sauvage, peaux rouge	a pure-blooded [American] Indian
Griff/Griffe	the child of a negre and a sauvage
Red bone, Sabine	an individual with tri-racial heritage or the descendant of one
Métis[se]	the offspring of a European and an Indian
Quarteron[ne]	a person with three white grandparents and one black grandparent
Pardo[a]	a light-skinned black person.
Sang-mêlé, Octoron[ne]	one-eighth African blood and seven-eights European blood
Quinteroon, Mamelouque	a very light-skinned person with approximately one-sixteenth African blood
Rouge, Cou rouge	a "red" person or "redneck"
Passe-a-blanc	a person with some black blood but sufficiently light-skinned to pass for white
Blanc[he]	a "white" person, of purely European descent

UPSTAIRS LOUNGE FIRE

---

29 *DEAD IN QUARTER HOLOCAUST*

"Fire Victims are Identified"

The States-Item Flash
June 23, 1973

POLICE today tentatively identified 13 of 29 persons killed by the worst fire in the modern history of New Orleans. The long process of trying to identify what was left after a fast-moving, 16-minute inferno left bodies stacked like pancakes in a French Quarter bar was assigned to a Charity Hospital team today.

Tentatively identified as victims of the fire, without addresses, are Leon Maples, Louis Broussard, John Goldring, Donald Dunbar, George Mitchell, Clarence McCloskey, Inez Warren, Joe Bailey, Guy Anderson, David S. Gary, Norman Lavergne, Kenneth Harrington and Jerry Gordon.

"We don't even know if these papers belonged to the people we found them on," Morris said. "Some thieves hung out there and you know this was a queer bar." Another police source said it is not uncommon for homosexuals to carry false identification, which could complicate the identification procedure.

Twenty-eight of the 29 killed were men and the place was packed for the weekly Sunday night beer bust, a kind of happy hour featuring all you could eat and drink for $2.

About 20 men were led to safety through a rear exit by a bartender, through a kind of theater and down a little-known fire escape.

Courtney Craighead, a survivor of the blaze, said he believes somebody dashed an inflammable liquid on the stairway and lit it. "The fire came up so fast," he said. "There was an immense smoke in the room immediately."

William White, 18, of Pineville, said he and Gary Williams, 19, also of Pineville, wandered into the bar while nosing around in the French Quarter. He said they might have stayed except for a bit of luck.

"There was a couple of guys quarreling at the top of the stairs," White said. "I don't like no kind of fights so we left. We weren't more than a block away when I looked back—the whole place was lit up."

THE HISTORY OF SLAVE TRADE

*The story of New Orleans is inseparable from America's heritage
of slavery. Historians estimate that over 100,000 enslaved Africans were
auctioned in pre-Civil War New Orleans, nearly a third of those children.
The everyday realities were absolute horror. But to begin understanding the
complex difficulties of modern-day New Orleans—the failures of Katrina,
prison populations, public housing—one must begin with the buying and
selling of human beings, and its common place in society, evidenced on this
page with an excerpted newspaper advertisement. Though this entry is
brief, this history is not, and we urge all readers to pursue it further at the
Historic New Orleans Collection and the Amistad Research Center.*

---

*60 VERY CHOICE SUGAR PLANTATION HANDS.
WILL BE SOLD AT AUCTION ON
TUESDAY, FEBRUARY 27, AT 12 O'CLOCK,
AT BANKS' ARCADE, MAGAZINE STREET*

BY J. A. BEARD & MAY. AUCTIONEERS.

ONE FAMILY.
1. JIM, aged 24, extra No. 1 field hand.
2. PHILLIS, his wife, aged 22, first rate hand.
3. ALECK, aged 23, extra No. 1 field hand, understands machinery,
   and boiler making, and has run centrifugal machines.
4. JOE KEY, aged 34, first rate field hand, cart and plow boy, very
   useful, understands machinery.

ONE FAMILY.
5. SUSAN, aged 24, good field hand.
6. CHARLOTTE, aged 8, ⎱
7. LONDON, aged 2,   ⎰ her children.

ONE FAMILY.
8. LEWIS, aged 47, good carpenter and sugar maker; a trusty and
   superior subject.
9. SALLY, his wife, aged 40, good field hand and hospital nurse,
   and is trusty.
10. SAM, aged 14, works in field and cart driver. [Excerpt]

THE SECOND LINE

New Orleans Jazz Club
July & August, 1950

To the Editor:

I want to tell you a true story. One hot, muggy night in June, 1902, a group of us, all boys, from the Hospital St. and Chartres St. section of New Orleans silently crept toward the rear of Saia's Stableyard but we bumped smack into the big smokestack of Seidel's furniture factory!

However, we finally found, via the moonlight, an empty stall, and we quickly arranged the washboards and tin cans and old zinc tubs....Then the two harmonica wizards of the 90's let loose with what we called "Cheer Up Mary". Poor old Mary surely got a dressing up that evening!

But something must have happened to Lula, the mule in the nearest stall, because as soon as we started playing Lula gave a wild snort and leaped clear over the chain bar. Meanwhile, from the chicken roost to the right of our newly acquired jam parlor, came a flutter of wings in all directions. Some of the chickens flew up on the shed, while some scattered over fences and finally into the street but the Tin Pan Serenaders never stopped playing. The two boys on harmonica were "Mexican" Piet and "Chinese" Pauly, respectively, and they were GOOD!!

The inimitable rhythm of the washboard, the tin kettle and the big zinc tub sounded like the coming of Jehova! All we needed was a long trumpet, and Moses could have added another commandment to the other ten. The noise was terrific. I still remember the big, leaky washtub before me. It's increditable, but our time was perfect; that 4/4 beat of later days never varied....Then came a barrage of old shoes, potatoes, watermelon rinds, finally a brick! We promptly retreated.

The quickest way out of the yard was over the back fence to Seidel's lumber yard, and out to Barracks St. Thus ended the first Jam Session of the Tin Pan Serenaders, later on the Regal Orchestra!

This group of 1902 grew and months later included Tom Early, Herbert Decueirs, Joe Pollizzi, Chink Marton, Alex Sposito, Bull Riley, Frank Otero, Wing Mazzarini, and myself. I doubled on cornet with Johnny Lala, in the Regal Orchestra. Emanuel Allessandro was on clarinet but he 'turned' classical soon after. Tots Blaise replaces Mazzarini on drums; Chink Martin joined Papa Laine's band and was replaced by Paul Venerella on bass fiddle. The late Leon Mello who stepped into Bull Riley's shoes was one of the best 'fake' trombonists, anywhere. He played on the order of our present George Brunis.

Without shaking peaches from anybody's tree, the famous Regal Orchestra, which had its inception in Saia's Stable in June 1902, and which later appeared in Quarella's Pavillion, in Milneburg, took no water from any other Jazz outfit of that period!!

Today, almost fifty years later, history doesn't know a single member of this group who struggled relentlessly to bring Jazz to the world!

Over-night critics and pseudo-historians who don't know a cornet from a bottleman's horn are the sole cause of this. Had we men and women to defend us like the fine group we have today in the New Orleans Jazz Club, the history of authentic Jazz of the 90's would be well known. A few of us still remain, the original jazzmen of the old guard. These musicians will always have a soft spot in their inner hearts for the New Orleans Jazz Club.

As their messenger, I say THANKS.

Johnny Provenzano,

1450 N. Villere St.,
New Orleans, La.

On February 21, 1948, a small, devoted group of jazz aficionados launched the New Orleans Jazz Club. Two years later, they began publishing a monthly bulletin, called *The Second Line*, typed-up with smart commentary, the latest jazz news and unabashed affection for the masters. For more, visit nojazzclub.org or the Hogan Jazz Library on Tulane's campus.

RIVER COMMERCE

All commodities shipped along the Mississippi,
from Baton Rouge, mile 236, to Mouth of Passes,
mile 0, in 2012. Measured in short tons.

TOTAL COMMODITIES	456,550,669
Coal, Lignite, Coal Coke	61,855,767
Crude Petroleum	32,250,276
Gasoline	17,265,668
Fuel Oil, Distillate/Residual	67,293,219
Fertilizers	20,875,854
Other Chemicals	31,722,381
Radioactive Materials	12,003
Forest Products, Rubber, Chips, Lumber	591,897
Soil, Sand, Gravel, Rock, Stone	15,105,671
Iron Ore and Scrap	8,084,658
Paper Products, Newsprint	242,905
Lime, Cement, Glass	2,279,104
Wheat, Corn, Grains	54,410,971
Peanuts, Soybeans, Flaxseeds, Oilseeds	62,124,846
Meat, Fresh and Frozen	352,969
Sugar	721,190
Coffee	264,080
Dairy Products	103
Alcoholic Beverages	105,956
Machinery and Equipment	1,660,139
Waste, Garbage, Sewage Sludge, Landfill, Waste Water	192,895

THE AINTS

Long before the "Who Dat" heroics of 2010, the New Orleans Saints were bottom-dwellers of the National Football League. The lowest point came in 1980, when 0-12, fans attended a home game wearing brown paper sacks over their heads. Not even star quarterback Archie Manning could save the "Aints" from a historically disastrous season.

Week	Opponent	Result
1	San Francisco 49ers	*L,* 23-26
2	Chicago Bears	*L,* 3-22
3	Buffalo Bills	*L,* 26-35
4	Miami Dolphins	*L,* 16-21
5	St. Louis Cardinals	*L,* 7-40
6	Detroit Lions	*L,* 13-24
7	Atlanta Falcons	*L,* 14-41
8	Washington Redskins	*L,* 14-22
9	Los Angeles Rams	*L,* 31-45
10	Philadelphia Eagles	*L,* 21-34
11	Atlanta Falcons	*L,* 13-31
12	Los Angeles Rams	*L,* 7-27
13	Minnesota Vikings	*L,* 20-23
14	San Francisco 49ers	*L,* 35-38
15	New York Jets	*W,* 21-20
16	New England Patriots	*L,* 27-38

NICKNAMES

- ↬ Nouvelle Orleans
- ↬ Nueva Orleans
- ↬ Great Southern Babylon
- ↬ Wet Grave
- ↬ Necropolis of the South
- ↬ Crescent City

- ↬ Queen of the South
- ↬ City that Care Forgot
- ↬ The Big Easy
- ↬ Chocolate City
- ↬ Hollywood South
- ↬ Who Dat Nation

SALTWATER FISHING

Species	Daily Limit [per person]
Red Drum	5 pp
Southern Flounder	10 pp
Spanish Mackerel	15 pp
Striped Mullet	100 lbs
Spotted Seatrout	25 pp
Blue Marlin	None
Sharpnose Shark	1 pp
Bluefin Tuna	1 per vessel per year
Yellowfin Tuna	3 pp
Grouper	4 pp
Red Snapper	2 pp
Lane Snapper	20 pp
Mutton	10 pp
Cubera	10 pp
Almaco Jack	20 pp
Greater Amberjack	1 pp
Hogfish	5 pp

BOUNCE

New Orleans' brand of hip hop combines chant-style shoutouts, a "Triggerman beat" and energetic call and response. Most critics agree that 1991's "Where Dey At" launched the genre. Below, a list of bounce artists.

Soulja Slim	U.N.L.V.	Choppa
Big Freedia	Katey Red	10th Ward Buck
Juvenile	Nicky Da B	Baby Erin
Magnolia Shorty	Partners-N-Crime	Magnolia Rhome
Ha Sizzle	Kane & Abel	Flipset Fred
Elm Boy Peg	Calliope Ceedy	Sissy Nobby
5th Ward Weebie	Cheeky Blakk	Da Stranger
Keezy Kilo	Lady Unique	DJ Duck
Lil Wayne	Jo Jackson	DJ Money Fresh

HANSEN'S SNO-BLIZ

Opened in 1934, Hansen's is the king of New Orleans sno-balls—home-made syrups generously drizzled over velvety ice. Not much has changed on Tchoupitoulas, including the patented ice shaver designed and built by founder Ernest Hansen.

U.S. PATENT 707,364
NOVEMBER 2, 1946

The present invention relates to new and useful improvements in ice shaving machines and more particularly to a power operated machine of this character including a rotary cutter for shaving a block of ice into substantially fine particles.

An important object of the invention is to provide a machine of this character including a manually operated follower for feeding the block of ice in a step by step movement toward the cutter.

An additional object of the invention is to provide a manually operated pressure plate for holding the block of ice against movement while being shaved and by means of which pressure is being maintained on the block of ice while being fed toward the cutter.

....

1. An ice shaving machine comprising a casing, an ice chamber in said casing, a rotary cutter journalled at one end of the chamber, a discharge spout leading from said end, a follower member in said chamber for advancing a block of ice longitudinally therein, an operating bar extending from said member, means for engaging the bar and moving the follower member toward the cutter, a plate hingedly mounted in the ice chamber for holding the block of ice against lateral movement, means for urging the plate from contact with the ice block, and means for moving and holding said plate in contact with the ice, said last means including a rod extending from said plate, an operating bar seated on said rod, a foot pedal, and flexible connecting means between said bar downwardly upon actuation of the pedal.

LE CODE NOIR

In 1724, the French government issued 54 articles of social regulation between whites, slaves, and free blacks of Louisiana. The harsh edicts remained law of the land until 1803. Below, excerpted selections from the Black Code.

I. Decrees the expulsion of Jews from the colony.

II. Makes it imperative on masters to impart religious instruction to their slaves.

V. Sundays and holidays are to be strictly observed. All negroes found at work on these days are to be confiscated.

VI. We forbid our white subjects, of both sexes, to marry with the blacks, under the penalty of being fined.

XIII. We forbid slaves belonging to different masters to gather in crowds either by day or by night, under the pretext of a wedding, or for any other cause...under the penalty of corporal punishment, which shall not be less than the whip. In case of frequent offences of the kind, the offenders shall be branded with the mark of the fleur-de-lys.

XXII. We declare that slaves can have no right to any kind of property, and that all that they acquire, shall be the full property of their masters.

XXIV. Slaves shall be incapable of all public functions, with powers to manage or conduct any kind of trade; nor can they serve as arbitrators or experts; nor shall they be called to give their testimony either in civil or in criminal cases; in no case shall they be permitted to serve as witnesses either for or against their masters.

XXVII. The slave who, having struck his master, his mistress, or the husband of his mistress, or their children, shall have produced a bruise, or the shedding of blood in the face, shall suffer capital punishment.

BIRDS OF NOTE

Species	Appearance.........Habitat
Mottled Duck	Brown feathers with yellow-orange bill... marshes and lagoons, like more famous mallard
Brown Pelican	Long, flat bill for plunge fishing...beaches and boat docks
Black Skimmer	Tuxedo look, cute underbite...sandbars, shallow inlets and estuaries
Roseate Spoonbill	Inspired shades of pink, "flame birds"... gregariously gathered in lakes and spillways
Clapper Rail	Rusty plumage, skinny bill...salt marshes, listen for summer rattling kek-kek
Least Tern	Eight-inch body, black and white...hovers over river, sandy shallows
Little Blue Heron	Solemn gray coat, black-tipped bill... freshwater swamps or insect hunting behind tractors
Tri-Colored Heron	Blue-gray head, white belly, red eyes... colony gatherings in swamp thickets
Red Knot	Pinkish coloring, size of a robin....winters on shallow coastlines
Ruddy Turnstone	White and black with orange patches... winters on sandy beaches
Seaside Sparrow	Palm-sized, yellow spot near eye...grassy marshes, listen for buzzy zeeee
Great Egret	Snow white, bright lores around eyes... clogged cypress swamp rookeries
Common Moorhen	Dark plumage, bright red nose stripe... dense wetlands with abundant vegetation
Glossy Ibis	Basic black-brown, though breeders have green shine...wetland generalist

MAPS

*Hand-illustrated maps to tell stories about classic
cooking, live jazz, city beauty, country adventures,
bar crawls, and the best of Mardi Gras*

CLASSIC CUISINE

LIUZZA'S BY THE TRACK

N LOPEZ ST.

Willie Mae's RESTAURANT

LIUZZA'S Lounge & GRILL

WILLIE MAE'S

SAINT ANN ST.

HAGAN AVE.

ORLEANS AVE.

PARKWAY BAKERY

DOOKY CHASE

CENTRAL
GROCERY

DECATUR ST.

Mississippi River

ROYAL ST.

CAFÉ
BEIGNET

90

COMMANDER'S
PALACE
RESTAURANT

COMMANDER'S
PALACE

WASHINGTON AVE.

⫸ CLASSIC CUISINE ⫷

*Where to find the Creole and Cajun signatures,
from beignets to turtle soup to crispy fried chicken.*

GUMBO
LIUZZA'S BY THE TRACK
A very dark roux layered with cooked-to-order seafood, locally-made sausage, okra and thirteen seasonings whose combination was concocted by owner Billy Gruber, who passed away in 2016. *1518 N Lopez*

....

SEAFOOD PO BOY
PARKWAY BAKERY
This century-old joint on the bayou has mastered the art of the fried shrimp po-boy. Eat it "dressed" with Zapp's chips and a cold bottle of Barq's. *538 Hagen St*

....

BEIGNETS
CAFÉ BEIGNET
Fried golden pockets lighter and chewier than their legendary kin at Café du Monde. Plus the line is way shorter. *334 Royal St*

....

TURTLE SOUP
COMMANDER'S PALACE
This dark, rich, soul-filling soup is made with real turtle meat, spinach and hard-boiled eggs. A drizzle of sherry is recommended. *1403 Washington Ave*

....

FRIED CHICKEN
WILLIE MAE'S
Fried to order, the chicken at this legendary 5th Ward lunch joint is served with shatteringly crunchy crust overlaying still-juicy meat. *2401 St Ann St*

....

MUFFULETTA
CENTRAL GROCERY
The old Sicilian grocery is the home of this local sandwich, layered with ham, salami, cheese and marinated olive salad on a Leidenheimer bun. *923 Decatur St*

....

RED BEANS & RICE
DOOKY CHASE
Historically, Monday was when women put the ham bone left over from Sunday to simmer in a pot of kidney beans. Go to Dooky Chase's for the matriarch Leah's flavorful take. *2301 Orleans Ave*

LOCAL EXPERT *Author Sara Roahen takes readers on a deliciously researched tour-de-fork in her 2008 book of essays,* Gumbo Tales, *published by W.W. Norton.*

⫸ MARDI GRAS ⫷

The insider's guide to February-March revelry, including
wig shops, float-maker dens and secret parade viewing spots.

MARDI GRAS WORLD

Warehouses near the Convention Center where Mardi Gras imagineer Blaine Kern makes his signature fantastical, grotesque parade floats for nearly all the super-krewes. Visitable! *1380 Port of New Orleans Pl*

BROADWAY BOUND COSTUMES

Feathers, sequins, marabou, jewels and glitter by the pound, a favorite of many Mardi Gras Indians looking to make their suits sparkle. *2737 Canal St*

CLAIBORNE UNDERPASS

Prime spot for elusive Mardi Gras Indian sightings on Mardi Gras, Super Sunday or St. Joseph's Day. The Backstreet Cultural Museum is another place to try.

FIFI MAHONYS

French Quarter wig shop specializing in custom hairpieces for Mardi Gras, from Marie Antoinettes to bouffants. Recently added a hair salon concentrating in flamboyant coloring. *934 Royal St*

CRESCENT CITY STEAKHOUSE

Crammed on Mardi Gras Day, as it's a favored spot for the last beef many people eat before Lent. *1001 North Broad St*

R BAR

Great viewing spot on Mardi Gras morning for the alternative, Bywater- and Marigny-based St Anne's parade, known for its abundance of elaborate hand-made costumes. *1431 Royal St*

ROYAL SONESTA

Annual "greasing of the poles" with Vaseline to prevent revelers from climbing up the poles to the hotel's balcony; celebrity greasers compete for prizes from a panel of judges. *300 Bourbon St*

> LOCAL EXPERT *No one knows Mardi Gras like fifth-generation New Orleanian Arthur Hardy. His best-selling* Mardi Gras Guide *and subsequent coffee table book are the next best thing to riding in Rex.*

MARDI GRAS

CRESCENT CITY
STEAK HOUSE

N. BROAD S

BROADWAY
BOUND
COSTUMES

CANAL ST.

CRESCENT CITY
STEAKS

ROYAL
SONESTA

BOURBON

MARDI GRAS
WORLD

PORT OF
NEW ORLEANS PL.

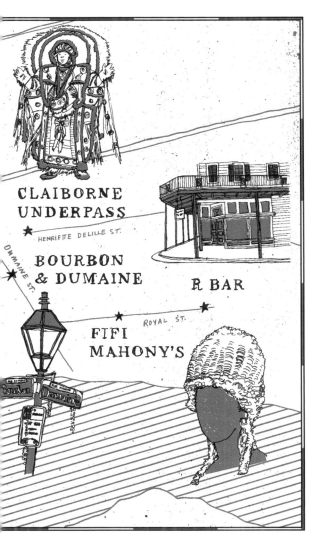

CLAIBORNE
UNDERPASS

★ HENRIETTE DELILLE ST.

BOURBON
& DUMAINE

R BAR

★ ROYAL ST.

FIFI
MAHONY'S

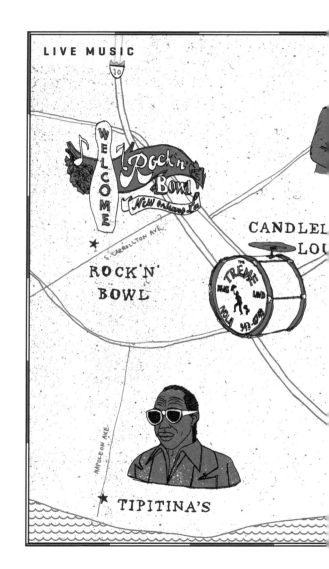

LIVE MUSIC

WELCOME

Rock n' Bowl
New Orleans La.

ROCK 'N'
BOWL

S. CARROLLTON AVE.

CANDLEL
LOU

THE
TREME
BRASS
BAND
NOLA
943-0778

NAPOLEON AVE.

TIPITINA'S

BROAD ST.

610

10

PRIME
EXAMPLE

ERTSON ST.

SIBERIA

SATURN
BAR

VATION
HALL

ST. CLAUDE AVE.

FRENCHMEN ST.

FRENCHMEN
STREET

ST. PETER ST.

FRENCHMEN

MISSISSIPPI RIVER

≫ LIVE MUSIC ≪

From a zydeco bowling alley to a rollicking weekly brass band to the world's sweetest jazz, NOLA's got the goods.

TIPITINA'S

Home of Professor Longhair until his death in 1980, now host to a mix of local and traveling bands. Often the site of surprise-guest, late-night sets during Jazz Fest. *501 Napoleon*

CANDLELIGHT LOUNGE

Wednesday night with the Treme Brass Band, a rollicking, mismatched 8-to-10-piece band playing for a good time. Order the "set up," a half-pint of booze, a bowl of ice and some plastic cups. *925 N. Robertson St*

SIBERIA

Known for metal but strays beyond to sissy bounce, singer-songwriter, rock and rap. Polish-Russian food from pop-up Kukhnya available in the back. *2227 St Claude Ave*

PRESERVATION HALL

Best place to hear NOLA trad jazz—acoustically, intimately.

This tiny institution is a venue, label, touring band and non-profit. No bar, but you can BYO in a geaux-cup. *726 St Peter St*

PRIME EXAMPLE

Best spot to catch contemporary jazz, from Jason Marsalis to Donald Harrison Jr. About 50 seats surround small tables. Fried chicken and yakamein served. *1909 N. Broad St*

ROCK N BOWL

Bowling alley-cum-dance hall. Thursday nights are best: start with a po-boy and wedge salad at Ye Olde College Inn next door, then join the boisterous zydeco crowd. *3000 S Carrollton Ave*

FRENCHMEN STREET

From the amazing schedule at Snug Harbor to the craft beer at DBA to no cover at the Spotted Cat, Frenchmen [though Bour-bonifying] is still the city's best place for high-quality tunes.

LOCAL EXPERT *Vinyl lovers have two legit outposts for record hunting—the legendary Louisiana Music Factory on Frenchmen and Euclid Records [ask for Lefty Parker].*

⫸ BEAUTY ⫷

*Lush landscapes, Creole patina and the
Great River make this city ever intoxicating.*

CITY PARK

Twice the size of Central Park, with America's largest grove of granddaddy oaks [one 800 years old] and a stunning sculpture garden valued at $25 million. 1 *Palm Dr, neworleanscitypark.com*

CAFÉ AMELIE

Opened less than ten years ago, the restaurant's draw is its lush Creole courtyard—the weathered-brick kind in your French Quarter dreams. *912 Royal St, cafeamelie.com*

ST. ROCH CEMETERY

Pronounced "Rock," visitors leave mementos for answered prayers—"ex votos"—and have since 1876, when the wrought iron gates first swung open. *1725 St Roch Ave*

MARIGNY OPERA HOUSE

The Catholic church that fell into disrepair after Katrina was reborn as a "church of the arts" in a soaring interior. *725 St Ferdinand St, marignyoperahouse.org*

GARDEN DISTRICT

Originally for Americans not keen on the Vieux Carré, this uptown hood is rich in shady streets, antebellum mansions and Commander's martini lunches. *Between St. Charles and Magazine Sts*

SONIAT HOUSE

French sugar barons built the Royal Street townhouses, the site of a 31-room boutique hotel famous for French antiques and morning biscuits. *1133 Chartres St, soniathouse.com*

ALGIERS FERRY

Because of low elevation, it's easy to forget about the Great River snaking through Orleans; the free ferry to the city's second oldest 'hood is the best view in town. *Canal St, nolaferries.com*

LOCAL EXPERT *Many point to one writer as creator of the dreamy notion of the Big Easy—Lafcadio Hearn—whose* Inventing New Orleans *anthologizes his widely read magazine articles from the 1880s.*

BEAUTY

★ CITY PARK

610

CAFE' AMELIE
★

ROYAL ST.

★
GARDEN DISTRICT

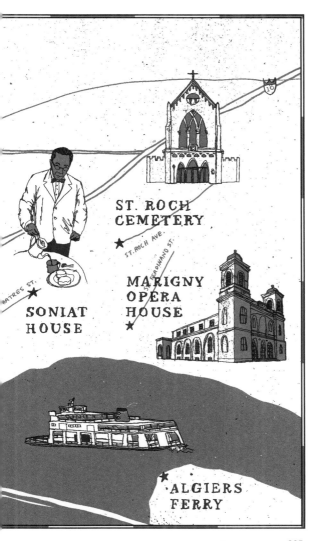

ST. ROCH
CEMETERY

ST. ROCH AVE.

FERDINAND ST.

DATRES ST.

MARIGNY
OPERA
HOUSE

SONIAT
HOUSE

ALGIERS
FERRY

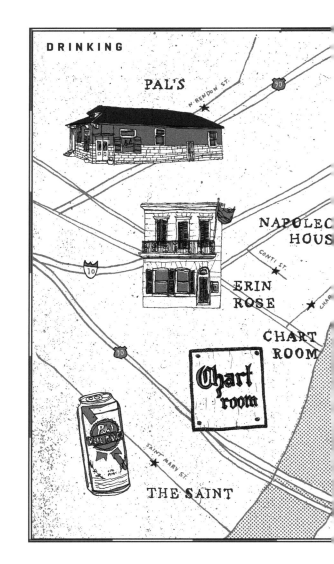

PAL'S

N RENDON ST.

90

NAPOLEON
HOUSE

CONTI ST.

ERIN
ROSE

CHART
ROOM

Chart
room

SAINT MARY ST.

THE SAINT

DECATUR ST.

★ CANE &
TABLE

MIMI'S ★

ROYAL ST.

POLAND AVE.

BACCHANAL ★

⟫ DRINKING ⟪

*Good time capital of America, whether you're rubbing
shoulders in a local's dive or classic cocktail den.*

ERIN ROSE

A rare locals' joint in the Quarter and late-night favorite for bartenders. Famous for Irish coffee, hot and frozen. Killer Po-Boys, the fantastic nouveau po-boy joint in the back. 811 *Conti St*

CANE AND TABLE

Hard not to imagine Hemingway's Cuba in this striking new spot with meticulously made daquiris. And the Creole courtyard is tops. 1113 *Decatur St*

NAPOLEON HOUSE

Touristy but that old-New Orleans atmosphere, the summertime refresher to order is the Pimm's Cup, complete with cucumber slice. 500 *Chartres St*

THE SAINT

Mellow dive transitions into late-night dance party. Happy hour til 9 includes buck-fifty PBRs and free jukebox plays. Bring your dog. 961 *St Mary St*

PAL'S

Platonic ideal of a neighborhood bar near the bayou. Midnight movies on Monday, cheap tacos on Tuesday, free food during Saints games. 949 *N Rendon St*

BACCHANAL

Opened as wine outpost in desolate area, now a bustling garden of mismatched furniture, live music and flowing rosé. Plus killer views of the barges and cruise ships. 600 *Poland Ave*

MIMI'S

Smoking, pool and beer in the high-ceilinged, red-tinted downstairs; no smoking, tapas and music in the cozy upstairs. A Marigny classic. 2601 *Royal St*

THE CHART ROOM

Quiet and dark with a great jukebox, *Esquire* called this map-lined French Quarter bar a "de facto oasis of sanity." 300 *Chartres St*

LOCAL EXPERTS *Find master bartender Chris Hannah in his white suit jacket at Arnaud's French 75. The only thing as good as the cocktail may be the story he can tell about it. 813 Rue Bienville*

≫ ACADIANA ≪

Roaming the Cajun backcountry for swampy landscapes,
real-deal zydeco and hours-old boudin.

THE BEST STOP

The roadside boudin kings
sell 2,000 pounds a day of their
pork links. Take some super
crispy cracklins to-go. C'est bon!
615 Hwy 93 N in Scott,
beststopinscott.com

....

OAK ALLEY PLANTATION

Take the slow route up-river to
see time-capsule plantations—
the drippy oaks and mansion
homes and leftover ruins of
slave heritage. *3645 Louisiana 18,*
Vacherie, oakalleyplantation.com

....

WHISKEY RIVER LANDING

Sunday dancing at Angelle's on
Henderson Swamp—doesn't
it just sound perfect? It pretty
much is. Afternoon zydeco in
the shadows of I-10. *1365 Hen-*
derson Levee Rd, Breaux Bridge

....

BREAUX BRIDGE

Small town perfection—Cajun
breakfast at Café Des Amis, culinary antiques at Lucullus, and

a night at the dreamy Maison
Madeleine. *breauxbridgelive.com*

....

SAVOY MUSIC CENTER

Handmade by local Marc Savoy,
these gorgeous accordions are
works of Acadian art, from the
bellows to the Italian reeds to
the Louisiana cypress. Saturday
jam sessions, too. *Hwy 190 W,*
Eunice, savoymusiccenter.com

....

HAWK'S CRAWFISH

Only open during crawfish season—December to May, dep-
ending—these folks purge their
mudbugs for 24 hours for hot-
plate, boiled perfection. *416 Hawks*
Road, Rayne, hawkscrawfish.com

....

FRED'S LOUNGE

Hooting, hollering and sidestep-
pin' to the French Cajun band
—all before 10 am on Saturday
morning—Fred's is a raucous
intro to backwoods Louisiana.
420 6th St, Mamou, 337-468-5411

LOCAL EXPERTS *Every October, the soul and heritage of Acadiana*
is celebrated in Lafayette during the 3-day gathering, Festivals
Acadiens et Creoles. festivalsacadiens.com

BREAUX
BRIDGE

WHISKEY
RIVER
★ ZYDECO

the Mississippi River

290

★

★ OAK
ALLEY
PLANTATION

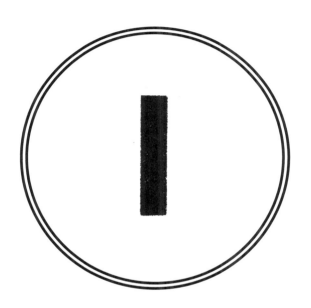

INTERVIEWS

Fourteen conversations with locals of note about running a restaurant, fixing a saxophone, charter schools, crowded prisons, a sportswriter's life and more

⟫ SUSAN SPICER ⟪

CHEF, BAYONA

IF SOMEONE ever asks me what to order, I'll always say sweetbreads. Just to test them.

CONFIDENCE is important.

WHEN I STARTED, I was five years older than half the cooks in my kitchen.

I DIDN'T HAVE an old Cajun grandmother. My mom was from Copenhagen.

THE BEST CHEFS dig the work.

I'M ONE OF seven kids and my dad was in the Navy.

A&G CAFETERIA. That was about it for eating out.

MOM HAD THIS set of mahogany bowls she would put the condiments in. Chopped eggs, scallions, peanuts, fried onions, chutney, all for her beef and curry.

I SHOWED A Culinary Institute brochure to my dad and he laughed. I was just aimless and looking for something.

I ALWAYS loved music—and musicians—but I had no talent.

TO GROW, to get better, you have to do what you don't think you can't do.

LIKE COMING back and putting on a comfortable pair of old shoes. The Big Easy, it feels good, comfortable.

WHEN I STARTED working for a chef, there was an epiphany.

I JUST SAID, finally, finally. This is satisfying everything.

I HAVE THIS New Yorker cartoon on my door. It's a woman chef standing at the table of a big-chested business man. "Oh, you're the chef? Well, my compliments anyway."

A FRENCH CHEF came in and said, "Your cooking reminds me of my grandmother." To me that was awesome.

AT THE END of the night, just give me my glass of wine.

≫ LESTER CAREY ≪

SIGN PAINTER

I WANNA GO draw the house that we stayed at in 1959. I wanna draw it before they tear it down. I'd never forget that address. 1910 St. Ann.

....

TOO MANY memories, you know.

....

MY MOTHER, she worked for white folks. She was a maid. My father worked on ships.

....

THEY HAD NO I-10. They had no cell phones. They had no Superdome. They had none of that.

....

I JOINED THE Army after Vietnam ended. My job was to bring the boys home.

....

I'VE BEEN drawing since I was 10 years old.

....

MOSTLY I PAINT signs. Meat specials for turkey necks, chicken wings, pig tails and tips, pork chops. Prices per pound. Cigarettes—liquor—beer.

....

I GET MY PAINT from the Home Depot.

MY FAVORITE SIGN is the one at Keller Market. Or the one at Melpomene and Magazine.

....

DURING KATRINA, I was walking across Claiborne and the water was up to here [pointing to his armpits]. I kept walking that way to the 'Dome. Then they evacuated us.

....

THEY HAVE many techniques you can apply to painting a sign. But I freehand because I'm an artist.

....

I USED TO BE at Jackson Square doing portraits. I like drawing, but there's more demand for signs.

....

I ALSO DO recycling. Fifty cents a pound for cans.

....

IF YOU MAKE a mistake, just white it out. Just roll it out white, let it dry, and come back and draw what it supposed to been.

....

OVER TIME, you develop a style. My style? I would describe it as improvisational.

⟫ MIKE LORINO ⟪

RIVER PILOT

THIRTY TO thirty-five ships a day. Some four football fields long and forty-five feet deep.

WE PILOT THE ships from the Gulf of Mexico to Pilottown.

I MET MY late wife when we were 14 and 15. Her name was Donna, and her father was a river pilot.

WE WERE married and I went down the river.

IT WAS MOSTLY sons that were getting in and I was a "son in law" so I was considered an outsider.

RIGHT NOW there's 47 of us.

THE ONLY WAY to get to our stations is by boat. It's marsh. No city, no nothing.

NARROW AND shallow. Both those things are hard for ships.

AND IN APRIL, the current goes to eight knots. All that snow up north comes right out the mouth.

WHEN I STARTED, you relied on the radio. And you looked out the window at the lights and knew where you were.

A LOT OF THE trees are gone. It's open water. Cypress, oak. They're getting all washed away.

LOUISIANA LOSES a football field of land every two hours.

THE ENVIRONMENTALISTS say that in 50 years the Gulf will be up to New Orleans.

DURING WORLD WAR II, two ships were torpedoed by subs just off Burrwood. The pilots could hear them come up and take on air. That's how close the Germans were to us.

THE BEST THING? Get on the lee side of the storm and ride it out.

YOU NEED A college education and pretty good nerves.

DO I FISH? No. I've had enough of the water.

»» MARTIN KRUSCHE ««

SAXOPHONE REPAIRMAN

I'VE ALWAYS been repairing instruments. I started with my own horn. I took my first sax apart before I could even play.

I WAS BORN in Munich and studied at a conservatory in Germany, but I moved here in 1995.

ONLY SAXOPHONES. I don't do clarinets or trumpets or flutes.

HERE IN New Orleans I am the guy everybody goes to.

BECAUSE I PLAY, I know the potential of an instrument and whether it's working as well as it can.

I MAKE MY living from two-thirds repair, one-third gigging.

SAXES MOLD to match their player.

THE VIBRATIONS have an effect on the inner structure. Over time, it shakes off the lacquer, becomes more and more resonant.

A PLAYED instrument is responsive and malleable.

JANUARY THROUGH April is my peak time. This is when Mardi Gras happens, Jazz Fest. Everyone's making money and getting their horn fixed.

A SAXOPHONE IS a woodwind, not a brass.

PEOPLE SEND horns from all over the country.

I LIKE Snug Harbor on Frenchmen. They cultivate a quiet room.

I REPAIR dents, broken springs, rusty parts, but ninety percent of what I do is pad replacement.

SOMEONE ALWAYS has an emergency. They just flew into town, dropped their horn on the flight, playing a gig that night.

A COMPLETE OVERHAUL costs $650. It takes a week.

YOU HAVE TO keep the player in mind. We do this now, we do the rest later.

≫ CALVIN DUNCAN ≪

SURVIVOR

MY MOM DIED when I was seven, so we bounced around a lot.

WHEN I WAS 14, I wanted to look nice in school, so I started shoplifting. That decision ruined my life.

I GOT CAUGHT and they took my mugshot.

A GIRL and a boy were at a bus stop on Esplanade and Roman. Two guys tried to rob them and winded up killing the boyfriend.

THEY PUT IT on Crime Stoppers, and someone called in and said the person who did the crime was a negro male named Calvin Duncan.

MY AUNTEE called me and said I was on the news. I said that couldn't be. She kept telling me I was, I was, I was.

I WAS 19 years old. And I had just started the process of joining the military. That was my dream.

THE STATE sought the death penalty. My trial lasted one day.

PROSECUTERS AND POLICE have the authority. They decide.

I DIDN'T KNOW what was going on. I wasn't educated.

MY FAMILY TESTIFIED to where I was on that night. I was at home painting the house for a birthday party the next day.

THE DETECTIVE in the case intentionally lied, and we eventually got the evidence to prove it.

YOU HAVE hope, you believe that things will work out. That they'll call your name and say, "We made a mistake."

EVEN AFTER you're found guilty, you believe the system will work itself out.

MY PROSECUTOR didn't agree with the Supreme Court that said he had to share exculpatory evidence.

I SPENT 24 years at Angola.

Twenty-three years I was an inmate lawyer.

....

WHAT GAVE THEM the authority to do what they did to me? The law.

....

THE POLICE department wanted $25 to send me a report. But you only making four cents an hour in prison.

....

WHAT'S THE ODDS of you getting those documents?

....

SISYPHUS WAS condemned by Zeus to roll a boulder up a steep hill, forever.

....

THEY SAY OUR court doors are open. That's bullshit. To get through all of them, you have to be Superman.

....

WHEN KATRINA hit, we weren't worried about the city. I was worried about my documents getting destroyed.

....

THIS ONE DA, his name is Jim Williams. He sent six people to Death Row and he had these trophies with their photographs on them.

....

TODAY, FIVE OF those six people are now free.

....

THERE'S A GUY, Reginald Adams, accused of killing a police officer's wife. And the same police officer remarried and had killed his second wife. Everybody knew. But Reginald was in prison for 34 years for it.

....

HE WAS released in June.

....

WHEN THE assistant prosecutor who prosecuted me became the judge over my case, the God of Hope left me.

....

HE SAID THAT I should have found the evidence 30 years ago .

....

GOD STEPS IN when the impossible needs to be done. Why he didn't do anything sooner, I don't know.

....

IN THE END, I still had to plead guilty to get out.

....

THAT'S THE system. I could continue to tell the truth and I might stay in prison, or say the magic words and I'd be out.

....

THEY GIVE you a $10 check when they let you out. I never cashed it.

....

ME AND MY daughter are close. She's 32 and she's in the Navy Reserves.

....

MY GRANDSON, his name is Josiah.

»» SANDY NGUYEN ««

COMMUNITY ADVOCATE

MY FAMILY came over from Vietnam in 1979.

THE DAY WE came, Dad got on a boat and became somebody's deckhand.

MY MOM STARTED shucking oysters within a week, and worked two, sometimes three shifts a day. My eldest brother, who was 10, took care of us.

I STARTED translating at 14. I did everything from court translation to immigration.

THE THREE main businesses in the Asian community are nails and fishing and grocery stores.

AFTER KATRINA, we formed Coastal Communities Consulting.

YOU KNOW THERE'S great seafood, but you don't know the people or the tough work behind the seafood.

WE HAVE OVER 1,200 clients, all commercial fishermen and surrounding businesses, like a gas station or the little bait shop.

THE VIETNAMESE, the Cambodians, the Americans—it's all the same. They all need the same type of grant assistance, loan help and business management.

ASIANS BUST THEIR tails to do this so that their kids can go to school and have a nice corporate job. The Americans, they hand down the fishing by generation.

AFTER THE SPILL, we saved people about $2.5 million in legal fees that they put back into their boats.

IT'S THE uncertainty, the not knowing. A lot of people got sick. You could see the stress in the fishermen.

I'M NOT A scientist or biologist, but I know the shrimp is not there like it used to be.

WHEN MY DAD retired, he sold his shrimp boat to my husband. So I'm a fisherman's wife too.

»» CATHY BADEAUX ««

MIDWIFE

I HAD A NATURAL childbirth. I was brought to a delivery room and my legs were put in stirrups, my arms tied down and they kept offering me an epidural.

BACK THEN PEOPLE were getting scopolamine, a hallucinogenic. It was the Twilight sleep.

YOU WOULD GET very violent during labor and not have any memories.

I STARTED MY training at Charity Hospital, working in Labor & Delivery up there on the 10th floor, where there were 1,000 births a month.

THE INDIGENT who went there, people with no insurance, which was a lot of people. It was not your best place to have a baby.

THREE OR FOUR mothers per room, yelling and screaming. Sick women, drug addicts, everything. It was natural birth whether you wanted it or not.

WOMEN WOULD SAY, go ahead and just deliver it if you want, and I would say, I would love to but legally I can't.

AS A NURSE, I was with the women while they were in labor. The physicians would come in and catch the baby.

IF I'M GOING to be with you when you have your baby, don't you want to know me a little bit?

I'VE DELIVERED thousands.

I COME HOME in the middle of the night and I have to sit here and unwind for an hour or two.

MY FAVORITE PART is when the head is crowning and the baby's about to be born. The end is when we really use our skills.

WHEN THEY SAY, "I don't think I can do this," I say, "But you are doing it."

WOMEN DON'T realize how strong they are.

THE MOTTO? Listen to Women.

⫸ VICTOR HARRIS ⫷

MARDI GRAS INDIAN CHIEF

I'VE WORN A Mardi Gras Indian suit for 50 years.

WHAT'S THE best one? The next one! You try to top that suit every year.

I WAS BORN into it. Being a kid, it was more exciting than Christmas.

THE CHIEF HAS to approve of you being in the tribe. Growing up, I had the legendary chief the late great Tootie Montana, just a couple of yards from me.

I WAS RAISED on Villere and Pauger Street.

FOR TWO, maybe three years, I sat around and watched them. I did little tedious things, but I never picked up the needle.

ONE DAY THEY told me, Come on, let's try and do this. I said, Man no, I don't think I can do that. He said, Oh, you been watching me long enough, it's time for you to start sewing. So that's how it all began.

THEN FOUR YEARS after, he said, Why don't you make you a suit?

MYSELF, I ALWAYS been a colorful person. Even in school I was always good at mixing and matching colors.

THAT WAS MY first suit, white with American eagles on it. Feathers, plumes, tips or fluff they call them, regular things, beads, pearls.

IN ORDER TO create my designs, I have to go to the spirits, to the elders, to the ancestors.

I THINK OF the African culture more than the Native Indian culture now.

ST. JOSEPH'S NIGHT and Mardi Gras Day are the two times we put our suits on.

NOWADAYS, they just jump up and down and say, I'm a chief. But they never worn a suit before. Those guys aren't respected. They haven't earned it.

I AM THE spirit of Fi Yi Yi. I truly believe in it. I don't mess with the spirits.

TRADITIONALLY we had to burn the suits, to give them back to the spirits. But I started saving them in the mid-80s.

I'VE GOT FIFTEEN or twenty at the Backstreet Cultural Museum.

THIS WAS segregation, so black people had their own Mardi Gras in their own community, and a lot of this was unheard of by tourists.

SPY BOY IS the person who's maybe two blocks ahead of the tribe, like a scout. He's looking for other tribes. Then you have the flag boy. He's a block behind the spy boy and a block ahead of the tribe. Then you have the wild man, he's just ripping and running, back and forth, making a lot of noise, whooping and hollering. They always find the craziest guy to be the wild man.

IN MY DAYS, when I saw the wild man coming, I used to run.

WHEN WE SEE another tribe, the drums go to beating. We're about to go into battle.

THE CHIEF is the chief. The chief is always the chief.

I DONE BEEN in a bunch of scuffles, but it's like a football game as far as I'm concerned.

CLAIBORNE AVENUE is the neutral ground. You used to have them big ole pretty oak trees until they came through with the I-10 and destroyed the land.

IT TOOK AWAY the Mardi Gras because that was Carnival for the black people.

PEOPLE JUST would go there and sit under those big ole beautiful trees. It was like every family had a tree, for picnics, for Sunday afternoon, for relaxation, whatever. That's how beautiful it was. And every family named a tree.

THAT WAS the place, that was the sacred ground. I'm telling you, everyone had a tree.

ONE OF MY major buddies recently passed away. He sat at the table with me for 47 years. I don't even know if I want to make it without him. We had a hell of a journey together.

PETER FINNEY

S P O R T S W R I T E R

THE FIRST heavyweight fight with gloves was here on Royal and Montegut. My grandmother saw it. September of 1892.

I GREW UP on Chartres Street, the 800 block.

MY FATHER ran a church supply company. All of his siblings became either priests or nuns.

HE FELL IN love with the girl next door. The Finneys were on Chartres, and next door were the Giacominos.

MY FIRST real job was covering high school sports at the *States*. That was the afternoon paper.

I MOSTLY worked on a typewriter. Later, there was the Portabubble.

YOU'RE A FAN, to a certain degree. But you try to keep your balance.

I PLAYED basketball at Loyola, and in the paper I would write, "Peter Finney did a great job!"

EVEN WHEN the Saints team was bad, the halftime shows were great.

ONCE THEY recreated the Battle of New Orleans. A cannon misfired and a guy lost his hand.

WE USED CARRIER pigeons that would leave Tulane Stadium uptown and carry the film to the roof of the *Times-Picayune*.

LSU'S GAMES with Ole Miss. Golf tournaments in City Park. Pistol Pete. We've been very lucky.

I GOT OFFERS to go to Chicago, Atlanta, Houston, Sports Illustrated.

THERE WERE a lot of "Aints" before the Saints came along. Twenty years before a winning season, forty years before they won the Super Bowl.

BUT THE Saints really pulled the city back together.

SPORTS HAS a special way of uplifting people.

ANGIE SHELTON

HOTEL HOUSEKEEPER

I WAS BORN in New Orleans.

MY MOTHER DIED when I was nine, so all seven of us went to go live with my grandparents on Burgundy between Toulouse and St. Peters.

MY GRANDMOTHER cleaned houses and had a restaurant on Bourbon.

AS KIDS, we had to work. We sold cans, newspapers, rags, bottled glass. Every morning at five o'clock, we'd go through the trash.

MY DAUGHTERS have it so easy.

MY HUSBAND has been on Bourbon Street for 37 years as a musician. He plays the bass guitar in the house band for Fat Cats.

I BEEN housekeeping manager at the hotel for 29 years. Two of my brothers work here too. Aaron and Farrell, the bellman and the maintenance guy.

WE DEAL WITH a lot of hair. There's hair on the bed or hair in the tub—that's the most frequent complaint.

HOW DO YOU know it didn't fall out your head?

THE HOTEL BUILDING used to be a morgue, and some guests claim to have seen ghosts.

A MAN KILLED himself in 226. Put blue tarp paper on the windowsill so we couldn't see in and shot himself in the bathtub.

I DO BELIEVE in ghosts, but I never seen anything here.

WE SEND OUT the comforters to be dry cleaned every six months. Should be every three.

IT DON'T TAKE a rocket scientist to clean. You just gotta be a clean person yourself.

ONE TIME a guy had a bowel movement, but he didn't flush. He complained and I said, "I thought you wanted to keep it, so we left it for you." Nobody's here to flush your shit.

»» GABRIELLE BEGUE ««

ARCHITECTURAL HISTORIAN

THE FIELD OF preservation combines everything I love.

DAD'S FAMILY came over from Southwest France in the 1870s. My great-great grandfather, Jean Begue, was escaping the Franco-Prussian War.

HE BECAME a butcher. His brother Hippolyte, a bartender.

THE GALATOIRE'S family is from the same part of France.

JEAN WON the lottery, $10,000 in Cuban gold, and his wife forced him to invest in real estate. He bought 16 buildings and built a few more.

THAT'S BEEN A part of my life forever, taking care of [my family's] buildings, all in the French Quarter and the Marigny.

OUR ARCHITECTURE comes from France, from Spain, from the Caribbean. How they're combined is what's unique.

OUR FAMILY owned a restaurant near the French Market called Madame Begue's. It claims to have invented brunch.

FOURTEEN COURSES. Drinking with every single one.

IT NEVER GOT fancy. It just became famous.

WE'RE A Galatoire's family. My parents were the people who came for lunch and stayed through dinner. Cesar was our waiter.

BEFORE MY parents bought it in 1978, our house was a brothel.

IT WAS CALLED House of the Rising Sun, not from *Easy Rider*.

WHEN MY MOM was very pregnant with me, she would still get guys ringing the door.

WE STAYED through Katrina.

I SAW ENTIRE tree branches just flying by, zipping past Elysian Fields into the Marigny. The sound of the wind was like a freight train.

⫸ DON RICHMOND ⫷

NEIGHBORHOOD HISTORIAN

MY NAME IS Don Richmond, and what else is it what you want? I don't hear well.

I CAME HERE because I read a book, *Fabulous New Orleans*, by Lyle Saxon.

MY GREAT-GRANDPARENTS came to New Orleans on their honeymoon.

THAT WAS IN the '60s. I lived in the French Quarter, in a building on Decatur Street.

IN THOSE DAYS, the Mafia were very much in evidence. They had bookie joints, they had prostitution, they had bars. You name it, they were in it.

EVENTUALLY, you pay a price for everything.

I BOUGHT THIS house [in Fauburg Marigny] in 1977. It was a ruin.

IT WAS BUILT, probably around 1825, by a woman whose name was Rosette Rochon, a free woman of color.

SHE WAS BORN a slave in Mobile, Alabama—her father was the first white shipbuilder there. Before he died, he freed Rosette's mother, a mulatto slave, and the children he'd had with her, and he gave all the children a heifer.

WHAT DO YOU DO with a heifer? You breed them. And Rosette became a businesswoman.

SHE OWNED a chain of grocery stores. She built houses. She was a licensed butcher. She loaned money, at interest.

IN 1863, she died after almost 100 years. New Orleans was bad, it was the Civil War.

THEY POURED the molasses in the streets to keep the Yankees from getting it.

IT WAS A man's world. For a woman, a so-called single woman, to succeed was a miracle. Rosette was exceptional.

⇉ LYNN RIVERS ⇇

TEACHER / SINGLE MOM

JUST 'CAUSE it works in New York doesn't mean it will work in New Orleans.

LOUISIANA HAS BEEN struggling a long time with education, period.

HERE'S HOW I see it: schools don't make people. People make schools.

I WENT TO John F. Kennedy High. It's no longer in existence.

MR. PARKER. He was a really good listener. That, to me, makes all the difference.

THE SYSTEM was more orderly back then. Things feel all spread out today.

I HAVE TWO daughters. Nine and seventeen. They go to KIPP Central City Academy and Warren Easton Senior High.

BY THE GRACE of God, we got in on the first try.

OUR DAYS START at 5:30 am.

OUTSIDE OF SCHOOL, my youngest attends NOLA Ballet, karate, the majorettes. My oldest is at the Trombone Shorty Academy at Tulane, too. How does they do it? Mama. That's how.

AN IDLE MIND is the devil's workshop. That's what the old folks used to say.

NO IPHONES at the dinner table.

YOU CAN'T prevent everything. But you better believe I'm going to try.

TAKE AN INTEREST in New Orleans culture. Because if you don't understand us, how can you teach our children?

SOME OF THE Teach For America teachers are great. Some, I wonder about the motives. Is teach-ing a calling, or are they thinking of paying off college loans?

THE GREAT Experiment. That sums up New Orleans education right there.

⇒ THOMAS STEWART ⇐

OYSTER SHUCKER

I'VE BEEN AT Pascal's Manale for 28 years—25 of them shucking oysters.

FIVE DAYS a week. Three in the afternoon until we close.

I'M AN ARIES. The day before I came in for the job, I checked my horoscope and it said, "You're coming to a job you're going to be at for a long time."

I STARTED OUT washing dishes.

THE CHEF ASKED me if I knew how to handle the knife. My mama taught me to never say you can't do something til you try. So I said, I'm gonna try.

I'M NOT A big fan of oysters. Never was. I don't dislike the taste, but it's just a texture thing.

I'D RATHER OPEN them and see other people enjoy them.

SEE THIS OYSTER? It's dead, lost all its energy.

I TAP ON them to see if they sound hollow. Then I feel for the opening at the front.

I USE THE Dexter-Russell with the plastic handle. I live by 'em.

THIS KNIFE FITS my hand perfectly.

SOMETIMES THEY snap in the heat of the moment, like the cereal, Snap Crackle Pop. I got two backups in case.

I FILE THEM about twice a week, very gently.

YOU DON'T WANT the knife to turn into an ice pick. I just want an edge so when I hit the muscle I get a clean cut.

I STILL WORK in the kitchen when they need me, but my main drag is shucking in the front.

WHEN IT GETS hot, I rub ice on my wrists to keep cool.

THAT TATTOO right there, that's my brand. Uptown T with two crossed oyster knives.

ESSAYS

*Stories from three local writers about classic city restaurants,
the true beauty of a cemetery, and one miracle during the
storm, plus short fiction from an American master*

⫸ MAKING A CLASSIC ⫷

Written by **BRETT ANDERSON** | **NEW ORLEANS'** iconicity leaves impressions even on those who have never visited. Before arriving, you've imagined the wrought iron casting its skewed-lattice shadows, the brass bands rounding corners in full blare, and the Creole cottages and shotgun shacks rising for blocks, some slanting ever so slightly in the sinking ground. It is all here, just as generations of culture dispatches and Tennessee Williams adaptations advertised, part of the daily sensory diet served up by a city whose reputation is so much bigger than it is in real life.

It is likewise that so many New Orleans meals unfold as you've already imagined they would.

The dishes you've heard about—save for jambalaya, which is less a restaurant dish than a staple of the home cook's stove—are all over the place. Gumbo is all but inescapable. Ditto po-boys, the mutable sandwiches that are always stuffed into long, locally baked loaves. You'll want to try barbecue shrimp, the buttery stew that has nothing to do with actual barbecue, and shrimp remoulade, a tart, cool shellfish preparation that sometimes comes in po-boys but is most often a palate-opening starter served over lettuce or fried green tomatoes.

The well of traditional New Orleans dishes on which the local cuisine built its identity is damn near bottomless when you consider how many are rarely [if ever] cooked exactly the same. This has much to do with the dizzying array of influences that have traveled through New Orleans kitchens. The port city's food contains the mark of Afro-Caribbeans, French, African-Americans, Sicilians, Spanish, Germans, Native Americans, French Canadians. Various combinations of these influences swirl through the Creole cooking of the city and the rural cooking of the Cajun bayous and plains, both of which are amorphous in their own right, having been picked apart by so many different New Orleans chefs of so many persuasions for so many generations.

This is food that is every bit as evocative as its reputation suggests. It is found everywhere from neighborhood dives and rough bar rooms to gilded dining rooms of the moneyed class, Parisian-looking albeit filtered through rye whiskey and/or seersucker, satisfying your expectation that New Orleans is America's "most European" of cities. All of this is true and, I believe, necessary information. It should help you enter into the thoughtful conversations that unfold wherever New Orleans food is served. That in turn will help you to navigate the magnificent mire without ending up with your spoon in a tourist trap's bowl of defrosted, factory-made gumbo.

But a word of caution about the above primer: It barely scratches the surface of the story about where New Orleans food came from. And that story itself tells you barely half of what you'll want to know about what is cooking in New Orleans today.

The colonial history, the preponderance of French words on menus, the tangle of class and race: These are just some of the tangible sources of New Orleans cuisine's celebrated *otherness,* all drawn from the boilerplate story New Orleans has been telling diners for generations. But more than anything, it is the city's status as a place that *requires* explaining, even to Americans, that is responsible for its foreign aura.

The city comes by this aura honestly, particularly where it comes to dining. Every restaurant worth visiting, and every dish worth consuming, has a backstory worth knowing.

THIS IS FOOD THAT IS EVERY BIT AS EVOCATIVE AS ITS REPUTATION SUGGESTS.

Teasing those tales into the open does not require much probing. Each New Orleans host may serve a slightly different menu, but all New Orleanians practice hospitality by decoding the city's mysteries for anyone who will listen.

The problem with New Orleans' always flourishing economy of opinion about itself—an economy I depend on to pay my mortgage —is that its wares are so often dressed as fact. And the problem with living in such a lively bazaar of "inside information" is the anxiety it creates among visitors and transplants to eat in the "right" restaurants, to avoid faux pas, to "fit in" among the natives—all of which flies in the face of the permissiveness that has always provided the cuisine its Technicolor sheen.

The cooking of southeast Louisiana came to be largely because its progenitors didn't cook anything like it was supposed to be cooked. Their legacy is a bastardization of food history and its attendant vocabulary.

New Orleans bordelaise has nothing in common with the sauce of the same name created in Bordeaux, where it is tinted red by the local wine and enriched with bone marrow. Not only is the local version clear, built from olive oil, garlic and herbs, it is most commonly found in restaurants of Sicilian ancestry. Likewise, the versions of trout amandine served at Galatoire's and Mandina's, both over century-old New Orleans institutions, would each be abominations to purists in the dish's French homeland, where the fish is never, as it is in New Orleans, fried.

The two restaurants sat atop the top of the list of places I determined I must try as soon as I moved to New Orleans in 2000 to become restaurant critic at *The Times-Picayune,* the city's oldest newspaper. I was far from an expert on the topic I was hired to master. I had visited New Orleans only once before. The advance intelligence I'd gleaned about Galatoire's and Mandina's, later confirmed by personal experience, suggested each provided a portal into separate quadrants of the same world.

Galatoire's, the boozy, jackets-required canteen of the establishment class, is to French-Creole cooking what philharmonic orchestras are to classical music, a guardian of tradition. Mandina's, with its Sicilian roots and saloon-like atmosphere, captures something just as old in amber from a different tree. It's a back-of-town joint that evolved from a corner grocery into a sandwich shop into a place a working person could drop into almost every night, for an Old Fashioned and a po-boy, and to place a bet with the bookie who also tended bar. Neither place was like anything I knew from growing up Scandinavian in the upper Midwest.

I could go on. Investigating New Orleans history through the prism of its restaurants is a field of academic study; a list of the ways the traditions vary from restaurant to restaurant could fill this guide. Together these guardians of the city's taste memories represent one of the world's great cuisines. Just about any New Orleanian will tell you that. It is our pride.

But the best evidence that New Orleans cuisine continues to evolve in the polyglot and rebellious fashion that gave rise to it the first place is not found in the restaurants that uphold its universally accepted history.

For that you need to be open to the idea of dining in restaurants like MoPho, a restaurant whose local-born chef fuses the indigenous cooking of New Orleans upper and working classes with the cuisine of Vietnam, whose immigrants long ago coalesced around strongholds in the suburban communities of the West Bank and New Orleans East. Bubble tea cocktails are served at the bar. Whole pigs are roasted out back. At MoPho, the Mekong and Mississippi deltas converge in a strip mall.

MoPho is at the vanguard of the "new New Orleans," a term born in the aftermath of Hurricane Katrina. Then it was how hearty but heartbroken locals referred to life in a disaster zone, when the few [and then countless] restaurants that opened, sizzling hamburgers and soft-shell crabs and red fish in the face of infrastructural collapse, provided the earliest inklings that the city could have a future that looked something like its treasured past.

Today the new New Orleans has abstracted into a more expansive phenomenon. It references the ways the post disaster city has not just bounced back but moved forward, spurred by a rebounding population, many of whom are young new arrivals of an entrepreneurial bent. And since progress begets change, a concept troubling to locals who love the city as they've always known it, the new New Orleans is not universally embraced.

New New Orleans restaurants don't follow the same scripts that even modern New Orleans restaurants wrote for themselves in the past. A rich sampling can be found in the lower French Quarter, in atmospheric gastropubs like Sylvain and Cane & Table, and downriver from there in the quickly gentrifying bohemian enclaves of the Faubourg Marigny and Bywater.

These days downtown New New Orleans restaurants tend to be the brainchildren of non-natives, or natives who've sought inspiration from untraditional sources. Mariza serves dazzling fresh regional Italian food beneath the loft apartments of a renovated rice mill. Kebab, inspired by street food found in Rotterdam and Berlin, serves fragrantly spiced lamb on housemade Turkish-style bread in what appears to be a bombed out storefront on St. Claude Avenue.

Bacchanal Wine & Spirits, a stone's throw from the Industrial Canal that broke through the levees during Katrina, is an old liquor store that transformed itself post-storm, slowly and for a time illegally, into something else entirely. It is a permanent pop-up restaurant, a genre it deserves some credit for inventing. Bacchanal is where you find the precise and careful cooking of Joaquin Rodas, a Salvadoran-American who was raised in Los Angeles, cut his teeth in Mexican kitchens and honed his craft during a years-long post-Katrina adventure in the modernist restaurants of Chicago. The food is served on disposable plates in a rough but lush urban garden. Live music plays nightly as ships pass above the rooftops, sliding across the Mississippi River that famously flows at a higher elevation than so much of New Orleans' settled land.

New Orleans lives in these and other new restaurants as surely as it does in its great temples of traditional gastronomy. The local debate over the merits of the latest breed will rage as long as the city is here, but whether or not they ever join the entrenched classics as accepted expressions of New Orleans' singular nature depends largely on whether or not you find the appetite to take their measure. The city's character radiates from its citizens, but its lifeblood comes from those who stand in awe of what they've created. There is no "right" way to find that vital spark that compels so many people to return, but you won't be in awe if everything you taste is precisely as you expect.

BRETT ANDERSON is the restaurant critic for *The Times-Picayune* in New Orleans. His writing has also appeared in a variety of national publications, including *Salon, Food & Wine,* and *Gourmet.* He has won two James Beard awards and has been anthologized in eight editions of *Best Food Writing.* In 2013, he was a Nieman Fellow at Harvard.

»» THE DEAD MUSEUM ««

Written by **RIEN FERTEL** | **IN NEW ORLEANS**, there is often more life in death than life in the living. T-shirts feature the lives of the recently deceased, while the newspapers' obituary pages rank second only to Sports in popularity. Funeral homes charge extra to construct dramatic, lifelike funeral poses: standing on two feet, for example, or seated in a garden with a cigarette and glass of champagne in hand. Neighborhood streets often fill with jazz funerals that dance the departed souls into the afterlife. Weather, termites, poverty, even plain old indifference all cause our houses and hospitals and schools and levees to succumb to a state of atrophy that some find frustrating, but most often describe as picturesque and charming. Famously, the city is gradually sinking, an inch annually in some neighborhoods, while the coastline gets nearer by the day. It might be said that we're slouching towards Hades.

The author William S. Burroughs understood the city's obsession with the departed. "New Orleans," he writes in Naked Lunch, "is a dead museum."

But nowhere do the dead remain more present than in the city's cemeteries. "A New Orleans cemetery," the distinguished local writer Walker Percy wrote, "is a city in miniature" that can often seem "at once livelier and more exotic" than the city's other architectural achievements: its renowned sidewalk corners, verdant gardens, and music clubs, which all jive and hum and bounce to their own life-affirming rhythms.

During its normal hours of operation, through frequent rainstorms and unremitting humidity, New Orleans's most notable city of the dead, St. Louis Cemetery No. 1, overflows with life. Visitors arrive by horse-drawn carriage, taxi, and rockstar-sized tour bus at the cemetery's front gates, where vendors hawk bottles of water and lemonade alongside guides offering unlicensed, not to mention dubious, historical expertise. Zombie-like clusters of thirsty tourists lurch along the cemeteries' main avenues and side paths to photograph and pose alongside the aboveground vaults, most of which are tall and boxy, constructed of brick and plaster, and adorned with a simple, marble plaque.

Towards the cemetery's center, women covertly lavish lipstick kisses on the future final resting place of Nicholas Cage—yes, that Nicholas Cage—who several years ago built a nine-foot tall, gleaming white pyramid amid a clump of crumbling, weathered crypts. In New Orleans, even the dead are not safe from gentrification.

Though New Orleanians have a deep and rich history of visiting cemeteries in order to feel more alive, the vaults at St. Louis No. 1— some of which date to the cemetery's 1789 founding—tend toward rot and decay. Families move away, die off, or, most typically, lose interest in visiting distantly-related, long-dead ancestors. The local Catholic Archdiocese refuses to pay for upkeep, unless a perpetual care plan has been purchased. Until recently, the cemetery operated in a sort of no-man's land, sandwiched between the French Quarter's seedy backside, the long-underutilized Armstrong Park, and the now former Iberville Housing Projects. A trip to the cemetery could quite literally result in death.

Rewatch the famous scene from Easy Rider, when Dennis Hopper and Peter Fonda take their French Quarter escorts on a post-Mardi Gras acid trip. Between the psychedelic freak-outs and nude bodies, the camera's eye pans up, over, and around a cemetery's tombs. Some are perfectly plastered, brightly whitewashed. But most suffer from various states of disrepair: sprouting with weeds and shrubs, brittle and broken, collapsing into themselves. This is St. Louis No. 1. And it looks very much the same now as it did in the late 1960s.

It is estimated that seventy-five percent of the tombs in St. Louis No. 1 are orphaned. Without caretakers, the vaults are easy prey to midnight marauders, tomb raiders of marble and trinkets and bone, disturbers of the afterlife. Perhaps even more detrimental to a vault's durability is the chimerical notion, regularly perpetrated by some tour guides, that scratching a series of three Xs into a tomb's soft mortar exterior will result in a wish made real.

The city's most famous tomb, as well as the likely ground zero of the triple-X scratchiti myth, belongs to Marie Laveau. Recently an unknown vandal painted the famous voodoo priestess's crypt a vibrant shade of pink. Whether practical joke or feminist art project, whimsy turned to angst when a local expert revealed that the latex-based paint would trap moisture inside, not allowing the vault's contents to "breathe," thus confirming that fresh air is not just for the living.

Once a month, about three dozen locals and visitors volunteer to spend their early Saturday hours tidying up the homes of the dead with Save Our Cemeteries, a nonprofit that has, since 1974, striven to preserve thirteen of the city's neglected historic cemeteries through fundraising and expert-guided walking tours. The organization's home cemetery is St. Louis No. 1, where they can be most visible, do the most good, and push back against a ceaseless tide of blight.

SAD AND SHABBY, THIS TOMB WAS MUCH MORE THAN AN ORPHAN. IT WAS NAMELESS.

One breezy and blue April morning, I was tasked, together with two other volunteers, with scrubbing the exterior of a particularly ramshackle vault with a gallon-sized spray bottle of mild soapy water and a soft-bristled brush, so as not to mar the fragile plaster walls.

But the tomb needed more than a good washing. It needed a full facelift. The vault's foundation and face were cracked with scars. Plaster peeling, its bricks exposed and turning to dust, the tomb colors that of desiccated flesh. Grass grew from its top and sides. What plaster did remain was decorated with so many XXXs that it resembled a cross-stitched quilt. Its marble plaque, designating who was buried within, had long been pried off and carted away—the resultant opening was crudely bricked over. Sad and shabby, this tomb was much more than an orphan. It was nameless, its anonymous owners lost to time.

I began to carefully scrub.

Though it felt entirely uplifting to volunteer a Saturday morning away, cleaning this rather unremarkable crypt selfishly clicked with the little niche I had begun to carve out for myself. In school classrooms and scholarly work, I teach and write about the chronicles of my city's past.

This volunteer opportunity was also a celebration of sorts, a chance to get outside, away from my writing desk, and just breathe. One month earlier I had successfully defended my doctoral dissertation in American History. My research focused on a now obscure literary circle from New Orleans, a close-knit community of nineteenth-century poets, playwrights, and pianists; novelists and journalists; historians and opera composers who promoted the idea that their city's past was exceptional, that their shared history made them different. They did not consider themselves French, though they principally spoke and wrote in that tongue. They were not impelled to call themselves Americans, yet they claimed United States citizenship and all the freedoms and failures this democracy entailed. Their tropical climate aligned more with the Caribbean than along the lines of their Confederate neighbors, while their nascent culinary and musical cultures were rooted in Africa.

They inhabited a historical and cultural middle ground, were an in-between people, exiles at home. And whether identifying as white or black or mixed-race, they often took for themselves the name Creole, a wide-ranging word derived from the Portuguese and used to designate a New World-born descendant of Old World peoples. In their writings, these Creoles imagined themselves a united community, a Creole City, a place defined by its own uniqueness. From Twain to Faulkner, Truman to Tennessee, most every ensuing writer who would come to embrace New Orleans and its people owed a debt to these now largely untranslated, unread, and forgotten authors.

Several prominent members of the literary circle were buried in this very cemetery, including its founder and spiritual godfather, Charles Gayarré. Born in 1805, the descendent of early French and Spanish settlers, Gayarré fancied himself a backwater aristocrat: an educated man, voluminous writer, and sometimes politician, born into a city where the inflated mortality rate—due to disease and violence— was inversely proportional to the population's literacy.

In a writing career that spanned eight decades, he penned novels, plays, and essays for major national magazines, but it was his several volumes of history that cemented his reputation as New Orleans's first and foremost man of letters. In his bestselling chronicles, he set out to encase the city's past in what he called "a glittering frame"; to inject life into history; to compose a semi-factual narrative brimming with gilded embellishments, poetic romanticism, and, at times, outright bullshit. And though he whitewashed history, fabricating names and events and dialogue, Gayarré's literary project worked. He wrote a history of this city that endures in the collective memory of its inhabitants.

Like any skillful biographer, I cultivated a knowledge of the man that could arguably rival what he knew about himself. I read his youthful writings and scoured archives for the rare unpublished jottings. I know

that at the age of twenty he fathered a son with a family slave. I possess the knowledge, loathing the fact, that he named the boy after himself, before cutting him loose and disavowing parentage for the remainder of his years. I know that he lost every penny after foolishly investing in the losing side of the Civil War. I know that he enjoyed a cup of hot chocolate in his old age. I know that it rained at his funeral.

But after spending my entire graduate student life with the man, Gayarré remained just words on a page. Alive and vivid and sharply meaningful, but still just ink. As I silently scrubbed this anonymous tomb, I imagined tracking down his mausoleum to find it in a similar state of decay. His vault would be grand, imposing, much like the life of the man whose remains it contained. But it would also be ravaged, forgotten, resembling so many other tombs scattered throughout St. Louis No. 1. By helping to restore his vault, I thought, I could get at the root of him. I could reach back into history and shake the hand of a dead man.

I scrubbed for three hours, until the XXXs had faded into the faintest of scratches. I asked Save Our Cemetery's then executive director, Angie Green, if she might know the location of the De Boré family plot—the tomb of Gayarré's mother's lineage—where I thought the man must be buried. She did not know, but told me to follow her.

We weaved through the cemetery's lanes, sidestepping tombs and tourists, searching for someone she described as St. Louis No. 1's unofficial sexton. Within minutes we ran smack into him.

He was a sturdily-built man, dressed in white paint-splotched overalls and carrying a stepladder, bucket, and long-handled brush. His face was red from long hours in the sun. We had caught him hustling from one tomb to another.

"Do you maybe know where Charles Gayarré, the historian, is buried?" I asked, before even learning the stranger's name.

"Know him?" he hollered in a sharp port of call accent that echoes in the voices of New Orleanians, "That's my cousin!" before offering up a big, spirited hand to shake.

Still nameless, he guided me towards the back of the cemetery, near but not crossing into the "Protestant Section," where Church law once dictated that the bodies of non-Catholics be laid to rest.

"Here he is," he proudly pointed. "Charles Gayarré."

The condition of the De Boré family tomb could not have been more magnificent. I ran my fingers across the plaster's fresh coat of white paint, glittering in the sunlight. Over the carved and weather-worn letters of its marble plaques, all intact and uncracked. And along the intricate filigree of its antique wrought iron fence and cross that guarded the vault's front, standing strong with the fine rust of age.

This was the handiwork of this same man, Ben Crowe, the Virgil to my Dante. He only recently resealed and re-whitewashed the tomb's façade, he explained, as he had so many vaults across this cemetery. I followed him next to a nearby tomb belonging to Pierre Derbigny, a French-born patrician who became one of Louisiana's first governors, that he had also meticulously restored. A decade ago, Crowe said, his dying mother informed him of their place as a distant branch on the Derbigny family tree. He didn't believe her at first. They were a working-class family from a working-class slice of New Orleans. Nearing retirement age, he maintained bridges for the railroad, and gave little thought to history. But he scoured genealogical records, tore through tattered volumes of history, and traced his family's local heritage back eleven generations, to some of the very founders of this city.

Crowe's ancestral tree flourished to include many ancient Louisiana families—Derbignys and Denises, De Borés and Lebretons —and he soon began wandering the alleys of St. Louis No. 1, searching for their final homes. Those tombs he found in disrepair, he re-plastered, repainted, rehabilitated. In his spare time and on his own dime, he soon began transferring his research, the hours spent exploring these ancient lives, onto graveside markers, hand-built but gallery-quality, complete with portraits and timelines. I wanted to ask a dozen questions, but Crowe had a tough time explaining his recent obsession with the past.

I'd like to think that New Orleans is a city validated by its own clichés. The bacchanalian atmosphere, the corrupt politics and police force, the omnipresent threat of violence that runs a thin red line down every street, the beautiful rot and exquisite decay— these hackneyed tropes have existed for three hundred years, because each reveals a glimmer of truth.

One last cliché might just ring true. Perhaps only in New Orleans do the dead—and undead—walk freely among the living, just as we, alive and full of spirit, move alongside the departed. For Charles Gayarré, Ben Crowe, and myself, the past tugs at every fiber of our being. Searching for life in death, we are all just chasing ghosts.

And sometimes we might find ourselves lucky enough to reach out and shake hands with the past.

I left Crowe with the promise to share my research and writing on his cousin Gayarré. He assured me that the next time he locates a relative's crypt broken and busted we will plaster and paint it together. With bucket and brush in hand, he disappeared behind a row of crypts to check on another family vault.

Before heading out of the cemetery gates, I stopped by my own adopted tomb, which now looked at least slightly cared for, and promised to visit it again.

RIEN FERTEL'S writing has appeared in *Garden & Gun* and *Oxford American*. His first book, *Imagining the Creole City*, will be published by LSU Press in late 2014.

»» LABOR AND RECOVERY ««

Written by **KATY RECKDAHL**

I WAKE WITH the sun streaming in. My baby is nine years old, and he lies with his head on my shoulder. He crawled in with me overnight.

I watch him sleep for awhile, getting sentimental about his round face and chubby cheeks, the knees on his long legs skinned from yesterday's scooter races around the block. Once we're both up, I help him get dressed in his school uniform, dark-green pants and a white polo shirt that he tucks in, hurried and lumpy, but enough to get him past the attendance monitor.

As we drive, down North Rampart, across the Industrial Canal lift bridge, I ask him about his birthday. I ask him how he feels when Uncle Richard says to him, "Hey there, Hurricane." And when Jacques introduces him during brunch, saying "I wanted you to meet Hector. He was one of the last babies born in New Orleans before the storm."

Hector looks over at me and rolls his eyes. "Mom," he says. "This isn't an interview."

Throughout my pregnancy, I rode my bicycle around town. It didn't take much effort to pedal my big purple cruiser, since New Orleans is a flat city, except for the levees that rise up on its edges. But at a certain point, other people got nervous seeing me on that bicycle.

I understand now. I saw a pregnant woman riding her bicycle recently and she looked precarious, maybe even idiotic. But, thinking back, nearly ten years now, I remember how comfortable it was. When I walked in the thick humidity, my big baby bulge weighed on my legs and sent rivulets of sweat tumbling to my skirt's thick elastic waistband. Not so on my bicycle, which gave me a breeze even on the most humid of summer days.

My friend Tammi Fleming, a public-health whiz, instructed me to never tell anyone that I was having a boy. "Make them guess," she said. The idea was that I would keep track of guesses. The first participant in Tammi's science project was Johnetta, who worked at the tiny pink launderette on Orleans Avenue and always stepped out the door to greet me as I biked home.

One day, soon after I started to show, Johnetta stuck her right hand out the door to wave, as she handed quarters to a customer with her left hand. "You're having a boy?" she yelled.

Lucky guess, I thought. But then no one was wrong. Not the clerk at the corner store, not the old Italian couple who ran the dry cleaners, not the men on the stoop in their electrician uniforms. From the way I was carrying, all round like a basketball, people said that they knew it was a boy. [The entire time, there was only one wrong guess, from a stone-drunk neighbor who stumbled up to me, felt my stomach and slurred. "Grrrl?" she said. Every single time I passed her, for the rest of my pregnancy, she was sure to correct herself. "Look at how high you're carrying," she'd say. "Definitely a boy."]

That's how it was, being pregnant in downtown New Orleans and riding your bicycle by the same people everyday, people who have known the baby's father all their lives. Here, what's personal can also be public.

Other musicians would warn Merv, my trumpeter boyfriend, that I could fall and hurt the baby. He wasn't really that worried about it. Sometimes, he'd laugh and roll his eyes and say, "You tell her." And they did. Constantly.

"LOOK AT HOW HIGH YOU'RE CARRYING," SHE'D SAY. "DEFINITELY A BOY."

Word got to Mama Rose Glasper, the widow of Papa Joe, who operated Joe's Cozy Corner. Joe's was the bar where I showed the bartender my ultrasound to explain why I'd refused the Friday-evening Crown Royal and 7-Up that he'd poured for me when he saw me roll up on my bicycle.

One morning, Mama Rose called me and asked me to stop by and get a container of her red beans, for the baby. Her red beans are always perfect: a nice tang of green pepper with a perfect amount of hot sausage. So I arrived that night on the bicycle. She told me it was my decision. But she'd feel better if I would please ride on the banquette, using the French word for sidewalk. "I would never forgive myself if that baby got hurt," she said.

A few days after that, I was carrying a round watermelon home in my front bike basket when the melon rolled to the side, tipping my bike tires into the air. I jumped down and caught myself, but the bike turned sideways and clattered to the ground at my feet. Rattled, I looked around to see if any of my lecturers were watching. After that, I started taking the bus to work.

In 2005, I worked as a reporter at an alt-weekly newspaper called *Gambit*, where the small edit staff was like a big family. That spring, I had covered a lot of issues about race and culture clashing. In neighboring Jefferson Parish, I followed a tip and walked to the back of the jail complex, where sheriff's deputies were practicing their aim at handmade wooden targets painted with brown faces with big white eyes and large red lips.

New Orleans police officers had angered the city's Mardi Gras Indians by turning their St. Joseph's Night holiday into almost a raid, where officers spun their cars through the park and ordered big chiefs to remove their "fucking feathers."

When the City Council had a hearing on the matter in July, a venerated big chief, Allison "Tootie" Montana, rose to speak and began recounting the police antagonism of the Indians. Then he said, "I want this to stop," and he collapsed from a heart attack. I bicycled around the chief's neighborhood and talked to his family and people who knew him best for my Gambit story. I also had been doing a bunch of freelance stories, to build up money for after the baby was born. So at eight months pregnant, I covered Big Chief Tootie's funeral for *The New York Times,* which meant walking along with the two-hour funeral procession, as brass bands and Indians with drums and tambourines played and sang in their chief's honor.

The baby moved around inside me that day whenever I got close to the tuba. That happened too, on Fridays. I usually would work through the first set of Merv's gig with the Treme Brass Band. But by around 9 p.m., I would walk into Donna's Bar & Grill on North Rampart Street. As soon as he saw me, Merv would call my favorite song, "Don't forget our Monday date. That you promised me last Tuesday." Merv was crooning and quipping and playing his horn with his bandmates and his son was moving along, in his own way.

Merv's stagename is Kid Merv because of his great-uncle, the great trumpeter Kid Rena, who began alongside Louis Armstrong in the Colored Waifs Home for Boys. Five years before, when I had met Kid Merv, he was in his brass-band uniform: white dress shirt, black tie, black pants, white brass-band hat. It was his birthday, so people had pinned money on his chest, as is the New Orleans tradition. I pinned a five on him, told him, "Happy birthday," and kissed him on the jaw.

A few weeks later, I saw Merv in Joe's Cozy Corner and he gave me his phone number. We dated, but inconsistently, because he struggled with drinking and with cocaine and went in and out of drug rehab. Finally a musicians' program in Los Angeles seemed to work. I was turning 40 that year and we decided it was time to have a baby.

Merv always wanted a boy and he always wanted to name the boy Mervin Junior. I was less enthusiastic about yelling Merv and having two people ignore me. We finally settled on the name Hector, for Merv's father, who had died when he was 12.

His full name would be Mervin Hector Campbell but we would call him Hector. Though to his uncle Richard, he would be known only as Hurricane.

About two weeks before my due date, during the last week of August 2005, I went to my weekly appointment. I was dilated a centimeter, which meant I could be moving toward labor. On the streetcar ride home, people told me that Hurricane Katrina, which had already hit Florida, was back over warm water in the Gulf of Mexico, building up for another landfall.

Soon, everyone I knew was preparing to leave town.

I'd evacuated the summer before, ahead of big Hurricane Ivan, which had turned at the last minute—as hurricanes so often do—leaving New Orleans with not even a raindrop. Like most everyone who fled Ivan, we experienced traffic so bad that a three-hour drive turned into a 12-hour nightmare. We drove with heavy eyelids, skipped meals rather than wait an hour in a fast-food drive-through, and stood in long lines for filthy filling-station restrooms with no toilet paper.

I couldn't bear the thought of going into labor in the backseat of a car stuck in evacuation gridlock. Merv agreed, saying delivering Hector himself was a no-go.

Besides, he said, we lived on Rampart Street in the French Quarter —high ground—and, if I went into labor, the city's hospitals, solid brick buildings, were some of the safest places to be during a hurricane. We decided to stay in New Orleans and take our chances.

I remember the next day like a home movie. I took a long bath, watched a doomsday news report about Katrina, and then plodded to Matassa's Market to get popsicles.

On some blocks, I had to walk in the street because so many French Quarter residents had pulled their cars onto sidewalks in front of their apartments to pack for evacuation. That was unusual. Many Quarterites took pride in not evacuating: the Quarter didn't flood and it rarely lost power for long because its below-ground electric lines, unique in New Orleans, were protected from hurricane-force winds.

New Orleans isn't known as a town run with military precision. But when a hurricane is approaching, people spring into action. I grew up in Minnesota, where you might have to grocery shop before a snowstorm and then huddle up inside with your gas-powered furnace until the storm was over and you were needed to shovel paths and dig out your car. But hurricanes require layers of preparation, far beyond wiring shutters closed or boarding up your windows.

To stay in town and do it right, you need candles, flashlights, radios, lots of batteries, charcoal for the grill, and drinking water. Sandbags, to keep water from flooding in the crack under first-floor doors. And gasoline, in case you need to evacuate. The night before, I'd been riding with a friend whose tank was three-quarters full, but he'd veered across three lanes of traffic to fill up when he saw a gas station that had gas in stock but no lines.

I'd gotten some D batteries and a jug of water. But I really wasn't in the mood to do all this preparation. I patted my stomach and told Hector we'd figure this out. Then I stopped to talk to my neighbors, old hands who were preparing for a payday. One had packed his ramshackle truck full of window-sized pieces of plywood and would work late into the night, hammering up all his boards. Another neighbor was doing a boom business, installing cable TV before the rain began. "Fill up the tub," he advised, so that I'd have water to flush the toilet if the water stopping running. I made a mental note about it. But honestly, I was still hoping that Katrina would turn away from the city.

When I got to Matassa's, I found them doing a brisk business: batteries, candles, and lots of booze. "If you go into labor soon, you might be able to get to med students down the street before they tap into the whiskey they just bought," the clerk quipped.

As I walked down the pasta aisle, I felt the first pain. Like the books said, it felt distinctly different, like a band tightening around me. I walked to the register where I ran into my friend, lifelong New Orleanian L.J. Gonzales, who was there buying cigarettes. "I am not leaving town, baby," he said with disdain.

L.J. is a free spirit with a high honking laugh but with regal manners, like he was teleported in from another century. So when I told him that I'd just had my first labor pain, he insisted on walking me home. I called the hospital, then Merv, who was at a gig. I called our friend Jeffrey, a tuba player who promised he would track him down.

But Merv didn't arrive for a few hours. L.J. insisted on staying until someone could relieve him and he gamely followed instructions, pressing on the small of my back during contractions. But I could tell that he was getting increasingly nervous, as he sat in my living room, carefully leaning out an open window to light up cigarette after cigarette.

Finally, my doula arrived and L.J. gave me a kiss on each cheek and nearly sprinted out the door. We were already in the car when Merv arrived, got in the driver's seat and drove like a bat out of hell while I perched on all fours in the back, since sitting was no longer possible.

By midnight, I was fully dilated. I started pushing, but Hector wouldn't come out. Everyone kept saying "push" but it wasn't working.

Turns out Hector's head was turned sidewise. All I could think was thank God we were not in a car somewhere. My OB reached inside me to turn him into position, which caused screeching pain. I begged for an epidural. Finally, in the wee hours of the morning, he came out, with a long skinny "banana head" from all the pushing. They rushed him to the recovery table, and I asked if I could hold him. "Let's make sure he's breathing first," said a nurse. My heart raced. Then I saw Merv, tears of joy cascading down his cheeks, as he stood over the table watching Hector's chest rise and fall with his first breaths. He looked at me and gave me a thumbs-up.

My work done, I slept most of the day. That evening, Merv weaseled in the hospital doors a few minutes after the hurricane curfew and confessed that he'd been all around town that day, bragging about our baby son.

The next morning, before dawn, the nurses woke us early. We were just getting the front edges of Katrina, but a hurricane-proof window had already broken upstairs. So they pushed all of our bevds into the hallway. A new mother across the hall starting screaming, a spine-tingling scream, because she'd been on the phone with her mom in the Lower Ninth Ward, who said it was already flooding badly and that she was in her attic. Then the phone had died.

Everyone looked nervous. I went to get Hector from the nursery and held him all through the storm, which sounded like an endless freight train. The power was out, but a battery-operated AM radio played at the nurses' station. Its air was filled with reports that made the city seem like the apocalypse. But we didn't see that. And whenever Merv went to the smoking area on a nearby roof, he got fairly accurate reports from staff about what was happening on the outside. We heard about the flooding. We heard there were fires and looting around town. We heard about the shelters crowded full of people in the Superdome and the Convention Center.

Despite that, we were happy with our beautiful boy, who was healthy, though hot to the touch, since there was no A/C and no windows that could open. We stripped him down to a diaper but he was still panting from heat. I also couldn't get him to nurse: Hector was not a natural and I was not either. Once it was pitch black after 8 p.m., Merv would light up my nipple with his cell phone so that I could try to connect it with Hector's mouth.

Late Tuesday, Giuliana, a nurse from the hospital nursery, convinced us that Hector would sleep better in the air-conditioned room they'd set up in a far corner of the hospital, one of the last sections with a working generator.

All that night, Giuliana was helping with airlifts, as a series of helicopters airlifted out the sickest people and babies. Early Wednesday morning, just after the city's water faucets went dry, one mother heard that all of the babies had been airlifted. We ran down empty hallways and up stairways in a crowd to the nursery, our hearts pounding. It wasn't true. But the line between truth and rumor was so thin in those days. I still can't explain most of that morning.

Merv came in from smoking and gathered all our things

together. He told me to grab Hector. Everyone had to leave now. There was a mob of thieves headed there to get the medicine in the on-site pharmacy, a nurse said. Doctors and nurses were going from room to room, telling patients to head to the parking ramp now. It was scary. I remember running in my slippers down the hallways, pushing Hector ahead of us in a clear plastic nursery bed.

Giuliana offered to give us a ride to Baton Rouge. There in the parking ramp, the nurses held an impromptu meeting, led by a head nurse who made sure that all other patients without cars had rides. She told us which route out of town had been cleared of storm debris, then warned that carjacking was rife. "Take off any visible jewelry and put it in your glove compartment," she said. "And, no matter what, do not stop for anyone."

As Giuliana put her car in drive, we were tense. But outside, it was quiet. Water lapped at the wheelwells, but the flooding was passable in Uptown New Orleans. The few people we saw were sitting on curbs at the edge of the street, their heads down.

It was the same way on the river bridge as we crossed it in the searing noon heat. No mobs. No one waving guns. Instead it was waves of trudging people, families with children and grandmas, in ragtag clothes, some still wet from wading through water. Those who couldn't walk were pushed in wheelchairs or even on rolling beds. Others pulled wagons or wheeled coolers with small children riding in them, followed by dirty dogs connected to owners by sagging leashes.

We searched the crowd to see if we could find our friend Jeffrey, a tuba player, and his family. I couldn't stop crying. As we drove out of the city toward Baton Rouge, we looked for the caravan of buses that were slated to take this same road into town by the end of that day. We didn't see a single bus.

On the way, we got our first cell-phone signal. I had barely any juice in my phone, so I called my sister Beth in Phoenix. She's a clutch in chaotic situations. "I'll call a travel agent and get you here to Phoenix," Beth said firmly. "Then I'll call Mom."

Beth said that Mom and Dad had been worried sick, glued to the TV, looking for us in every New Orleans report. That morning, they had been debating driving their minivan from Minnesota to New Orleans, to pick us up at the hospital. Beth laughed. "But don't call now. She won't hear the phone, because she's drying her hair, getting ready for all the news reporters that are headed to the house to talk about you."

Soon Beth called back, breathlessly. "You're booked for a flight from Baton Rouge to Phoenix on Friday—it's the best we could do," she said. "Can you wait at the airport until then?"

It was Wednesday. I felt smelly and ratty as we stood in the airport reservations line with Hector and our "luggage," a light-blue hospital trash bag. The man in front of us paid for his flight from a wad of bills. At the next counter, a woman tried to pay with a series of credit cards, none of them working. But Beth had come through. We checked in two days early. The reservations clerk advised us to head to the gate.

When we got to security, a woman looked down at the baby seat and frowned, then walked from the scanner to me. "How old is that baby?" she asked. I panicked, remembering something about infants not being able to fly until a certain age.

"He's three days old," I said. "We just came from the hospital in New Orleans."

She nodded, then motioned to everyone ahead of us in line. "Everyone—please move out of the way," she said. "There's an infant here." I told her thank you and she touched my arm. "When you get to the gate, sit down," she said. "Your color looks awful."

The gate crew saw Hector and got us on the next plane to Atlanta. On the connecting flight to Phoenix, the pilot announced that there was a new Katrina baby from New Orleans on board that night's flight and everyone applauded.

None of us remember rain while we were in Phoenix. It seemed like outer space there, with the soaring red cliffs and the canyons, the dry air that left your nose feeling like it had dried glue inside. We spent nearly a year out west. A lot of that time is blurry to me now. Hector's erratic feeding and sleeping schedules. Negotiating with FEMA and Red Cross and finding loved ones. Our phones were nearly worthless. The building that controlled the 504 area-code for cell phones had been submerged, Sometimes you could get a daytime call, but usually it was too jammed. Often we'd get late-night calls, relaying word that someone else was out of New Orleans and safe. Or not.

My sister Beth shuttled us around and fed us at first. Within the first few weeks, Valley Presbyterian Church in Scottsdale called to sponsor us, setting up an apartment furnished with everything from pots and pans to a handmade baby quilt to a pair of slippers for me next to the bed. Merv's bandmates from the Treme Brass Band also ended up in Phoenix, thanks to the same church and a jazz group. Fred Sheppard, a gangly older saxophonist who had played with Otis Redding, Ray Charles, and Fats Domino, spent hours holding Hector, who was always content with Shep. Turns out Shep would scat in his ear to calm him.

The tuba player, Jeffrey, and his wife Ann ended up living by us in Scottsdale. As we crossed the river bridge on that Wednesday, they had been walking through floodwaters to the Convention Center; they had left on foot two days later when the children became so dehydrated that they were shaking. A renegade city bus driver stopped on the bridge, opened her doors, and drove them and a busload of other evacuees to safety a few hours away.

Jeffrey's Scottsdale house had a pool, but the closest his son would go was a lawnchair at its edge, where he'd sit with his little Spiderman towel.

Merv also seemed shaken by the storm in a way that I couldn't understand. It was as though he felt invincible, beyond sobriety. People bought him drinks as a way of welcoming the new trumpeter from New Orleans and he eagerly gulped them down.

I no longer saw his gigs. Hector was going through a colicky time and I often spent hours walking the neighborhood like a zombie, lulling him to sleep. A few hours later, Merv would undo my work, as he stumbled in, loaded and loud.

Merv still had penitent moments, but I was done. On Mother's Day, I had the locks changed. I applied for a year-long, post-Katrina journalism fellowship and I got it. A month later, my friend Munce flew into town to help me pack up a car and a U-Haul trailer on my own. We rode back toward New Orleans in a caravan with Jeffrey and Ann and their family. Merv stayed behind.

We drove for 12 hours at a time, up and down mountains in Arizona and then across the width of Texas. Hector hated his carseat then and screamed whenever he wasn't sleeping, unless someone sat next to him. So Munce drove almost non-stop.

Early in the drive, as we drove up a steep Arizona incline, a car sidled next to us and pointed to the U-Haul trailer hitch, which had come loose and was hanging by one wire. Jeffrey bought wire and a chain from a nearby gas station and fixed it by the side of the road.

The next day, Jeffrey's big rental truck stalled in the middle of the mountains. U-Haul brought us a new one hours later, but we had to unload and reload the whole thing in the middle of an asphalt parking lot.

Finally, 11 months after we'd left, we drove back into New Orleans. My friend Carol had been staying at my place on Rampart while her roof was repaired, so our apartment was clean and felt like a time capsule, ready for the infant who no longer fit the clothes laid out for him.

Munce took a cab to the airport, back to Minneapolis. I put Hector in the stroller and took a walk through the French Quarter, back to Matassa's, where owners Louie and John Matassa greeted him like their own child.

At that point, nearly a year after the storm, Hector was one of the few babies in town, a novelty of sorts. I'm not a punctual person, but during that time, I had to leave the house about 20 minutes early so that I could give people time to grab Hector's chubby leg in the stroller or—if I knew them—to hold him and kiss him on his cheek.

My neighbors concluded that Hector had basically planned the whole thing. "Have you met Hector?" they'd ask someone new. "He was born up at Touro just before the storm. He was determined to be a New Orleans baby."

Jeffrey's family had settled for the time being in Houston, near some of Ann's family. He would commute to New Orleans to play gigs on weekends and would sleep on my couch. But it was several months until I saw the rest of the Phoenix crew again.

It was a somber meeting, a funeral for Shep, who hadn't told anyone he was sick and was found dead in his Phoenix apartment. I wrote the paper's obituary for him, my vision blurry with tears. His ashes were flown to New Orleans for the funeral service, which ended —as is the custom for musicians—with a large traditional second-line procession. His niece walked out front holding a framed photo of him with his saxophone, his gray hair puffing out from under his trademark leather baseball cap.

I carried Hector through the procession. It was raining lightly, and New Orleans evacuees who had driven to the funeral from all parts of the South were following the band, dancing and monkeyshining for Shep. He may have died alone, they said, but he wasn't going to be put down alone.

Hector couldn't stop watching the drummers. He'd fuss whenever I turned away from the drumline, often to hug someone whom I hadn't seen since before the storm. When we got back to the church, Fatman, a snare drummer, handed Hector his drumsticks as a gift. As rain dripped onto us, Hector stood on the ground and reached toward Fatman's snare. Tap tap tap.

Fatman was overjoyed: I remember his big grin as he walked us to the car, with Hector still drumming even as I strapped him into his car seat. Then Hector tapped the sticks on the back of my headrest, all the way home to Rampart Street.

KATY RECKDAHL'S work has appeared in *The New York Times*, the *Christian Science Monitor*, *The Weather Channel*, *The New Orleans Advocate* and *Louisiana Weekly*.

⟫ THE KINGDOM OF GOD ⟪

Written by **WILLIAM FAULKNER** | **THE CAR CAME SWIFTLY** down Decatur street and turning into the alleyway, stopped. Two men alighted, but the other remained in his seat. The face of the sitting man was vague and dull and loose-lipped, and his eyes were clear and blue as cornflowers, and utterly vacant of thought; he sat a shapeless, dirty lump, life without mind, an organism without intellect. Yet always in his slobbering, vacuous face were his two eyes of a heart-shaking blue, and gripped tightly in one fist was a narcissus.

The two who had got out of the car leaned within it and went swiftly to work. Soon they straightened up, and a burlap bundle rested on the door of the car. A door in the wall near at hand opened, a face appeared briefly and withdrew.

"Come on, let's get this stuff out of here," said one of the men. "I ain't scared, but there ain't no luck in making a delivery with a loony along."

"Right you are," replied the other. "Let's get done here: we got two more trips to make."

"You ain't going to take him along, are you?" asked the first speaker, motioning with his head toward the one lumped oblivious in the car.

"Sure. He won't hurt nothing. He's a kind of luck piece, anyway."

"Not for me he ain't. I been in this business a long time and I ain't been caught yet, but it ain't because I been taking no squirrel chasers for luck pieces."

"I know how you feel about him—you said so often enough. But like it was, what could I do? He never had no flower, he lost it somewheres last night, so I couldn't leave him to Jake's, going on like he was for another one; and after I got him one today I couldn't of put him out nowheres. He'd of stayed all right, till I come for him, but some bull might of got him."

"And a-good thing," swore the other. Dam'f I see why you lug him around when they's good homes for his kind everywhere.

"Listen. He's my brother, see? And it's my business what I do with him. And I don't need no–that wears hair to tell me, neither."

"Ah, come on, come on. I wasn't trying to take him away from you. I'm just superstitious about fooling with 'em, that's all."

"Well, don't say nothing about it, then. If you don't wanta work with me, say so."

"All right, all right, keep your shirt on." He looked at the blind doorway. "Cheest, what's the matter with them birds today? Hell, we can't wait here like this: be better to drive on. Watcher say?" As he spoke the door opened again and a voice said: "All right, boys."

The other gripped his arm, cursing. At the corner two blocks away a policeman appeared, stood a moment, then sauntered down the street toward them. "–here comes a bull. Make it snappy now; get one of them fellows inside to help you and I'll head him off and keep him till you get unloaded." The speaker hurried off and the other, glancing hurriedly about, grasped the sack resting upon the door of the car and carried it swiftly through the doorway. He returned and leaned over the side of the car, trying to lift up the other sack onto the door. The policeman and his companion had met and were talking.

Sweat broke out on his face as he struggled with the awkward bundle, trying to disengage it from the floor of the car. It moved, but hung again despite his utmost efforts, while the body of the car thrust against his lower chest, threatened to stop his breathing. He cast another glance toward the officer. "What luck, what rotten luck!" he panted, grasping the sack again. He released one hand and grasped the idiot's shoulder. "Here, bub," he whispered, "turn around here and lend a hand, quick!" The other whimpered at his touch, and the man hauled him half about so that his vacant, pendulous face hung over the back seat. "Come on, come on, for God's sake," he repeated in a frenzy, "catch hold here and lift up, see?"

The heavenly blue eyes gazed at him without intent, drops of moisture from the drooling mouth feel upon the back of his hand. The idiot only raised his narcissus closer to his face. "Listen!" the man was near screaming, "do you wanta go to jail? Catch hold here, for God's sake!" But the idiot only stared at him in solemn detachment, and the man raised up and struck him terribly in the face. The narcissus, caught between fist and cheek, broke and hung limply over the creature's fist. He screamed, a hoarse, inarticulate bellow which his brother, standing beside the officer, heard and came leaping toward him.

The other man's rage left him and he stood in vacant and frozen despair, when vengeance struck him. The brother leaped, shrieking and cursing, upon him and they both went to the pavement. The idiot howled unceasingly, filling the street with dreadful sound.

"Hit my brother, would you, you—," panted the man. The other, after the surprise of the assault, fought back until the policeman leaped upon them, clubbing and cursing impartially. "What in hell is this?" he demanded when they were erect and disheveled, glaring and breathless.

"He hit my brother, the—"

"Somebody certainly done something to him," snapped the officer. "For Pete's sake, make him stop that racket," he roared about the deafening sound. Another policeman thrust through the gathering crowd. "What you got here? Mad cow?" The idiot's voice rose and fell on waves of unbelievable sound and the second policeman, stepping to the car, shook him.

"Here, here," he began, when the brother, breaking from the grasp of his captor, leaped upon his back. They crashed against the car, and the first officer, releasing the other captive, sprang to his aid. The other man stood in amazement, bereft of power to flee, while the two officers swayed and wrestled with the brother, stretching the man, screaming and kicking, between them until he wore himself out. The second policeman had two long scratches on his cheek. "Phew!" he puffed, mopping his jaw with his handkerchief, "what a wildcat! Has the whole zoo broke out today? What's the trouble?" he roared above the magnificent sorrow of the idiot.

"I dunno exactly," his partner shouted back. "I hear that one in the car bellow out, and look around and here's these two clawing in the gutter. This one says the other one hit his brother. How about it?" he ended, shaking his captive.

The man raised his head. "Hit my brother, he did. I'll kill him for this!" he shouted in a recurrence of rage, trying to cast himself on the other prisoner, who crouched behind the other policeman. The officer struggled with him. "Come on, come one; want me to beat some sense into you? Come on, make that fellow in the car stop the howling."

The man looked at his brother for the first time. "His flower is broken, see?" he explained, "that's what he's crying about."

"'Flower?'" repeated the law. "Say, what is this, anyway? Is your brother sick, or dead, that he's got to have a flower?"

"He ain't dead," interjected the other policeman, "and he don't sound sick to me. What is this, a show? What's going on here?" He peered into the car again and found the burlap sack. "Aha," he said. He turned swiftly. "Where's the other one? Get him quick! They've go liquor in here." He sprang toward the second man, who had not moved. "Station house for yours, boys." His companion was again struggling with the brother, and he quickly handcuffed his captive to the car, and sprang to the other's aid.

"I ain't trying to get away," the brother was shrieking. "I just want to fix his flower for him. Lemmego, I tell you!"

"Will he quit that bellowing if you fix his flower?"

"Yeh, sure; that's what he's crying for."

"Then for God's sake fix it for him."

The idiot still clutched his broken narcissus, weeping bitterly; and while the officer held his wrist the brother hunted about and found a small sliver of wood. String was volunteered by a spectator, who fetched it from a nearby shop; and under the interested eyes of the two policeman and the gathering crowd, the flower stalk was splinted. Again the poor damaged thing held its head erect, and the loud sorrow went at once from the idiot's soul. His eyes were like two scraps of April sky after a rain, and his drooling face was moonlike in ecstasy.

"Beat it, now," and the officers broke up the crowd of bystanders. "Show's all over for the day. Move on, now."

By ones and twos the crowd drifted away. And with an officer on each fender the car drew away from the curb and on down the street. And so from sight, the ineffable blue eyes of the idiot dreaming above his narcissus clenched tightly in his dirty hand.

Before publishing his first novel in 1926, **WILLIAM FAULKNER** resided on Pirate's Alley in the French Quarter, where he wrote short fiction for local newspapers.

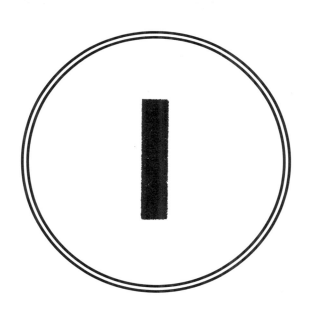

INDEX

❯❯❯ INDEX ❮❮❮

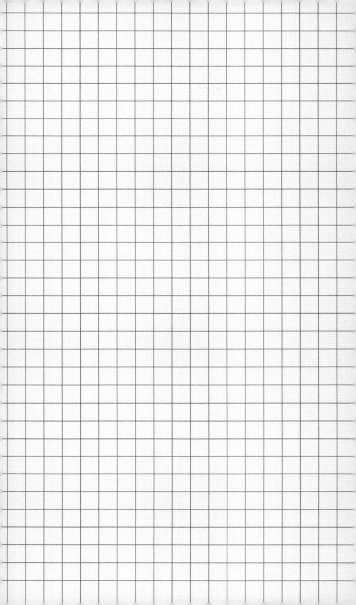

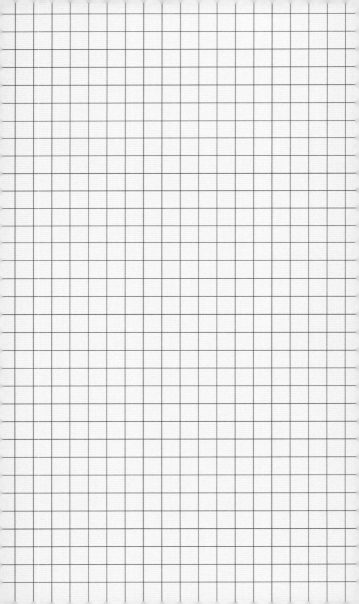